The
Church Today

Paul W. Powell

D1435846

ANNUITY BOARD
OF THE SOUTHERN
BAPTIST CONVENTION

Dedication

To Thomas E. Miller, Jr.

Managing Director — Public Relations Division

A valued partner in ministry

Table of Contents

Introduction

The church is the only movement Jesus left on this earth to represent him. Anyone who wants to be on the cutting edge of what God is doing in the world today needs to be vitally involved in a local New Testament church. Jesus intended it to be the primary way of evangelizing the world, edifying believers, and ministering to the needs of humanity.

We better understand the nature of the church by looking at the analogies for it in scripture. The church is variously called the bride of Christ, the body of Christ, the family of God, the army of the Lord, and the building of God.

A bride is a woman to whom a man commits himself. So the church is people to whom Christ is committed. A body is an organism through which a person acts. So the church is people through whom Christ works. A family is a group of closely related individuals who nurture and care for one another. So the church is people whom Christ nurtures. An army is a band of soldiers armed and organized for war. So the church is people with whom Christ advances his kingdom. A building is a structure in which a person dwells. So the church is people in whom Christ dwells.

The idea of a bride suggests our relationship to Christ; the idea of a body suggests our work for Christ; the idea of a family suggests our fellowship in Christ; the idea of an army suggests our mission from Christ; the idea of a building suggests our unity with Christ.

As a bride we should be loving.

As a body we should be serving.

As a family we should be nurturing.

As an army we should be advancing.

As a building we should be standing.

Beyond our common commitment to Jesus Christ as Lord there are certain beliefs that are non-negotiables. What are they? We believe the Bible is the word of God — that the Old Testament and the New Testament are two lips through which God speaks to us today. We believe in soul competency — that each person has the capacity to know and respond to God on their own. We believe in the priesthood of the believer — that each person is capable of, and responsible to, approach God for himself/herself. We believe in soul freedom — that we must be free from all human interference in responding to God as we understand him.

The church, like all movements, must have leaders. So, God gave two leadership offices to the church — pastors and deacons. To these chosen people he assigned the specific responsibilities of caring for the spiritual and physical needs of his people.

Christ is the center and the circumference of our faith. To better guarantee that we would always stay on center in our faith, the man who cared little for ritual or ceremony gave to his church two rituals to observe. One, baptism, is to be initial in our Christian experience. The other, the Lord's Supper, is to be continual in our Christian experience. The purpose of both is to anchor us to him — his death, his burial, and his resurrection. As long as we observe these two ceremonies correctly, we can never drift far from the core of our faith.

Christ loved the church and gave himself for it. We should do the same. We cannot give ourselves for it vicariously as he did. But we can give ourselves in ministry, service, and loyalty. I am not suggesting a replication of the first century congregation, but we are to let the twenty-first century congregation be the Body of Christ. It is to be guided by God's word, evaluated by God's word and modeled after the spirit of the living word, Christ himself. This book is a call to commitment to Christ and his church at the deepest level of your life.

— Paul W. Powell

Chapter 1

The Church Jesus Built

Matt. 16:18-19

"If you destroyed all the churches tomorrow," George Bernard Shaw once said, "people would the very day afterwards begin to build them back again. That's true because the church stands for something vital and essential."

The church gains its significance, in part, because it is the only movement Jesus left on earth to represent him and to which he committed the work of extending his kingdom. It, like nothing else other than the Bible, has the stamp of divine approval upon it.

Since this is true, you might expect Jesus to have spoken of the church often. Actually there are only two instances recorded in scripture where Jesus used the word "church." The first record is in Matthew 16:18, and the other is Matthew 18:17.

In the second of these instances he spoke of the church as the supreme court to settle disputes among believers. If two Christian brothers have a difference they cannot reconcile privately, Jesus said, "Let them tell it to the church" for final arbitration (Matt. 18:17).

In the other instance, the most familiar one, Jesus said, "...upon this rock I will build my church; and the gates of hell shall not prevail against it. And I will give unto thee the keys of the kingdom of heaven: and whatsoever thou shalt bind on earth shall be bound in heaven: and whatsoever thou shalt loose on earth shall be loosed in heaven" (Matt. 16:18-19).

The occasion for this statement was Jesus and his disciples coming to the coast of Caesarea Philippi. There he asked his disciples, "Whom do men say that I, the son of man, am?"

The disciples responded by sharing the street talk about him. Some were saying he was John the Baptist, others that he was Elijah, and still others were saying that he was Jeremiah or one of the prophets. Jesus then asked his disciples life's most important question, "Whom say ye that I am?"

Peter was the first to respond. He said, "Thou art the Christ, the son of the living God."

Jesus acknowledged Peter's deep spiritual insight and reminded him that it was God, not man, who had revealed this great truth to him.

Following this, Jesus told his disciples that he must go to Jerusalem where he would be betrayed, crucified, buried, and raised again the third day. Sandwiched between these discussions of his identity and his destiny is this marvelous teaching concerning the church.

The Greek word translated "church" is the word *ekklesia*. We get our word "ecclesiastical" from it. It literally means "the assembly" or "the called out ones." In the Old Testament it referred to the congregation of Israel, the people of God who were called out of Egyptian bondage. Among the Greeks it signified primarily an assembly of citizens in a democratic state. Greek cities were self-governing, usually through a town hall meeting. When the meeting was set, notice was given to the citizens and those who attended constituted the assembly. The city was governed by those who heard and answered the call to be a part of the assembly. Gradually the word took on a Christian meaning until it referred to an assembly of God's people. When Jesus used the word "church" in these two instances, he was referring to those who had heard and responded to God's call to salvation and service.

As Jesus spoke of the church in Matthew 16:18-19, he used three symbols: rocks, keys, and gates. The rocks speak of the foundation of the church. The keys suggest the function of the church. And the gates refer to the future of the church.

From these symbols three truths emerge about the church Jesus built.

- First, it is founded on a great truth (v. 18a).
- Second, it is commissioned to a great task (v. 19).
- Third, it is destined to a great triumph (v. 18b).

The Church's One Foundation

First, the church is founded upon a great truth. Jesus said to Peter, "Upon this rock I will build my church..." It is clear that the church is founded on the rock, but who or what is that rock?

These are perhaps the most critically examined words in all the New Testament. What do they mean? There are three common interpretations. Some believe the church is founded on Peter, the man. The first time Jesus met Peter (John 1:42) he gave him a new name. He told him that hereafter he would not be called Simon, but "Peter," which means "a stone" or "rock". So some believe Peter was the first head of the church and that his successor, the Pope, is the vicar, the direct representative of Jesus Christ on earth today.

Others believe the church is built on Peter (and the other apostles) as an example of redeemed, transformed humanity. They suggest that the change of Peter's name indicates a change in his character and that the church is founded upon transformed lives. The Bible does teach the church should have a regenerate membership, but that is not, I believe, the thrust of this verse.

The best understanding of this statement, in my opinion, is that the church is founded on Peter's confession, the divinely revealed truth that Jesus is the Christ, the son of the living God. To put it another way, the revelation is the foundation.

What we have in Jesus' statement is a play on words. The name Peter is the Greek word *petros*. The word Jesus uses for rock is *petra*. Petros is masculine in gender. Petra is feminine. Petros means a pebble, a small throwable stone. Petra means a mass, a great ledge of rock.

So, the church is not built upon Peter the man or upon Peter the example, but upon the truth of Peter's confession. It is built on the divinity of Jesus Christ.

The essence of Christianity is this: Jesus Christ is God. He is not just sent from God; he is not just a part of God; he is not just a representative of God; he was and is God. Upon that foundation Christianity and the church rests.

Once Philip said to Jesus, "Lord, show us the Father, and it sufficeth us." Jesus responded saying, "Have I been so long with you, and yet hast thou not known me, Philip? He that hath seen me hath seen the father" (John 14:8-9). And Paul declared that in Christ all the fullness of deity dwells in bodily form (Col. 2:9).

If you're looking for God, you can stop your search right now. God has come into the world. He has become one of us. His name is Jesus of Nazareth. You need no other God besides him. You can pray to him. You can worship him. You can entrust yourself, your body and soul, to him. And if you do, you will live eternally in his presence. He is the foundation of the church. It is built on him.

Some people try to build their church on the pastor. But when he fails or moves, the church falters. Others try to build their church on programs — music or recreation or youth. And when they go flat, the church declines. But the only solid foundation on which to build is the person of Jesus Christ.

We sing, "On Christ, the solid rock, I stand, all other ground is sinking sand ... all other ground is sinking sand." The scriptures confirm this. Paul said, "Other foundations can no man lay than that is laid, which is Jesus Christ" (1 Cor. 3:11). And Paul wrote, The household of God ". . . is built upon the foundation of the apostles and prophets, Jesus Christ himself being the chief cornerstone" (Eph. 2:20).

When plans were being made for the Empire State Building, skeptics said, "It can't be done. You can't erect 102 stories of concrete and steel, one on top of the other, and expect it to stand."

But the engineers replied, "If we can make the foundation deep enough and strong enough, there is no limit to the height we can erect the building."

The years have proven that the foundation of the church is deep enough and strong enough to withstand the storms of time, for it is founded on the divinity of Jesus Christ.

Our Reason for Being

Second, the church is commissioned to a great task. Jesus said, "I will give unto thee the keys of the kingdom of heaven: and whatsoever thou shalt bind on earth shall be bound in heaven: and whatsoever thou shalt loose on earth shall be loosed in heaven" (Matt. 16:19).

The idea of keys suggests the function of the church. In Luke 11:52 Jesus accused the Pharisees and Sadducees of destroying the "key of knowledge." He accused them of not entering in themselves (into the kingdom) and of hindering those who were.

Keys, you know, represent access to, or opportunities. They have reference to the gospel, which, by preaching, we offer people access, the opportunity, to salvation. Our mission, then, is to shed abroad the knowledge of the son of God so that men and women everywhere, by believing in Christ, can enter into eternal life.

The second half of this verse is complex and interesting, "Whatsoever thou shalt bind on earth shall be bound in heaven and whatsoever thou shalt loose on earth shall be loosed in heaven." The best translation is, "whatsoever you shall bind on earth must be that which has already been bound in heaven" and "whatsoever you shall loose on earth must be that which has already been loosed in heaven."

You remember in the Lord's prayer Jesus taught us to pray, "Thy will be done on earth as it is in heaven ..." We must do here on earth that which the Lord has already proposed, determined, willed in heaven. Or, to put it another way, the purpose of the church is to do the will of God on earth. And God's will is that none should perish but that all should come to repentance (2 Pet. 3:9).

Many churches today are suffering an identity crisis. They don't know who they are or why they are here. They are like the church Vance Havner once described. He asked the preacher, "How are you getting along?" The preacher replied, "We are living in idolatry — just sitting around admiring our new church. We have arrived: we have it made — no more worlds to conquer."

Then he added, "What ought to be a milestone has become a millstone. We have run out of goals. We have lost our sense of mission."

The church that loses its sense of mission is in peril of its life. The church exists by mission as a fire exists by burning. Let a fire cease to burn and it becomes ashes. Let the church cease to be missionary and evangelistic and it ceases to be a church — and the coldness and dullness of death sets in.

The result is that many churches have more fashion

than passion. They are more pathetic than prophetic. And they are more superficial than sacrificial.

Many ministers are keepers of the aquarium instead of fishers of men. They are happy to be baby-sitters for believers suffering from chronic malnutrition. We must ever be careful lest we build large sanctuaries that serve as million dollar launching pads for sending up Roman candles.

Do you want to know why so many of our churches today are in turmoil? Listen to Lyle Schaller, well-known church consultant: "The parish without a truly divine purpose, the church without a sense of direction, or the congregation without an understanding of mission can turn committed Christians into frustrated critics."

World evangelization is not, nor can it be, the pastor's pet project. It is God's strategy for the ages and his whole body must be involved in it.

The Winning Side

Third, the church is destined to a great triumph. Jesus said, concerning his church, "... and the gates of hell shall not prevail against it" (Matt. 16:18).

The Greek word for "hell" is the word Hades, which means "the grave, the place of the dead." The word "prevail" comes from two Greek words meaning "strength" and "down on." The idea is that even death does not have the power to bring the church down.

Even as Jesus spoke these words the shadow of the cross was falling across his path. Dark and foreboding days lay ahead. In his next breath he would tell his disciples he must go to Jerusalem, suffer many things of the elders, chief priests and scribes, be killed, and be raised again on the third day (Matt. 16:21).

Jesus was saying he would die, but the church would live on. The gates of hell would not prevail against it. One by one the apostles would die, all of them as martyrs for their faith, but the church would live on. The gates of hell would not prevail against it. Throughout history, the persecution has continued. But the blood of the martyrs has become the seed of the church. And the workers have died, some naturally and some violently, but the work has gone on. The gates of hell have not prevailed against it.

I hope you don't suffer from the illusion that the bloody butchering of Christians stopped with the conversion of Constantine or that the persecution of Christians has almost ended. If you do, you are wrong. Figures are not easy to come by, but evidence is mounting that martyrdom is a painfully contemporary reality. In many countries, Christians pay a dear price for believing. According to the World Christian Encyclopedia (Christianity Today, March 19, 1990, pg. 12), one in every 200 workers on the mission field is killed. And an average of 300,000 Christians a year are martyred around the world. Attorney and human rights author Nina Shea says more Christians have died for their faith in the twentieth century than in the previous nineteen centuries combined (Baptist Press, Dec. 13, 1996). Yet Christ's church lives on.

The church is like a nail. The harder you hit it, the deeper you drive it into the hearts of men and the soul of society.

Jesus didn't say his church would face no opposition;

he said it would suffer no defeat. There are always enemies — some Pharaoh on our trail, some Jezebel to hound, some Goliath to taunt. And the last enemy we shall come up against is death itself. And when death is finally dead, the church will be there to conduct its funeral service.

From the early 1800s China was a prominent mission field for Presbyterians, Methodists, Baptists, and other denominations. Operating colleges, schools, and hospitals, as well as churches, great progress was made in winning many Chinese to Christ.

However, in 1949 Mao Tse Tung came to power and almost immediately missionaries were *persona non grata*. The cultural revolution under the Communists was vigorously anti-intellectual, anti-Western, anti-religion. The radical Red Guards destroyed libraries and hymnals, burned Bibles, and profaned houses of worship. Ministers were ridiculed and forced into manual labor or exiled to remote communes. Most missionaries were forced to leave the country.

For 35 years the doors to China were closed. Among those missionaries expelled was Dr. Wiley B. Glass, the father of Eloise (Mrs. Baker James) Cauthen. Dr. Cauthen was president of the Foreign Mission Board of the Southern Baptist Convention for a quarter century. Dr. Glass returned from China to Southwestern Baptist Theological Seminary, where he taught missions. One day, after teaching a class dealing with missions in China, Dr. Glass was walking across the campus of the seminary. The student who told me this said he approached Dr. Glass and said to him, "Dr. Glass, it must be hard to see all your work in China destroyed."

Dr. Glass stopped, pulled himself up to his full six feet, four inches, and said, "Young man, I'll have you know when Jesus went to China he went to stay."

In recent years the doors to China cracked open to the West and we were allowed to peek inside once again. The startling fact we discovered is the church has not simply survived under Communism, it has flourished. In spite of the absence of missionaries who had traditionally assumed leadership, without the use of church buildings, with few available Bibles and almost no Christian literature, the church has not just been preserved — it has been multiplied.

During the period of Communist persecution the number of believers in China doubled to a total of 4 to 5 million. It is estimated that there are now 6,000 churches in China and churches are reopening at the rate of one or two per day. In addition, it is estimated that there are 50,000 house churches, informal groups of five, ten, or fifteen believers meeting in private homes to study and worship.

Incidentally, the same kind of thing has happened in Russia. For 70 years the scriptures were all but banned in the Soviet Union. It is estimated from 1917-1986 only 450,000 Bibles were allowed in the country through legal means. But today, after the new age of "glasnost," begun under Mikhail Gorbechev, the Bible is permitted, but the supply can't keep up with the demand. It is estimated that as many as 100 million copies of the scriptures are needed to satisfy the needs of Christians and inquisitive non-Christians among the 150 million people of Russia. In Russia today the church lives and so does the Bible.

All of this is but a confirmation of what Jesus said,

"The gates of hell shall not prevail against my church."
No matter how dark the night, no matter how severe the
persecution, the church will stand. The last enemy we
shall face is death, and when death is no more, the church
will be there.

Dr. Glass was right — when Jesus went to China he
went to stay. And his church went to stay, also. An unknown poet expressed the truth this way:

> *O, where are kings and empires now,*
> *Of old that went and came?*
> *But Lord thy church is praying yet,*
> *A thousand years the same.*
> *Unshaken as the eternal hills,*
> *Immovable she stands.*
> *A mountain that shall fill the earth,*
> *A house not made with hands.*

The person who links his life with Christ and his
church is therefore linking his life with that which is eternal. In spite of occasional appearances, the church is on
the winning side.

The Nature of the Church

Chapter 2

The Church, His Bride

Ephesians 5:22-33

A group of motion picture engineers classified the following as the ten most dramatic sounds in the movies: a baby's first cry; the blast of a siren; the thunder of breakers on rocks; the roar of a forest fire; a fog horn; the slow drip of water; the galloping of horses; the sound of a distant train whistle; the howl of a dog; and the wedding march.

They found the sound that causes more emotional response and upheaval than any other is the wedding march. It has the power to bring forth almost every emotion: sadness, envy, regret, sorrow, tears, as well as supreme joy.

I suppose it is because marriage is the deepest and most intimate of all human relationships that the Lord uses it as an analogy of his relationship to his church. Thus, the church is often referred to as the bride of Christ.

The idea of the relationship between God and his people as a marriage goes far back into the Old Testament. Again and again the prophets spoke of Israel as the chosen bride of God (Hosea 2:19-20; Is. 54:5; Jer. 3:14).

27

And the marriage symbol continues through the New Testament. Jesus is referred to as the bridegroom both by himself and by John the Baptist (Matt. 9:15; Mark 2:19; Luke 5:34; John 3:29; Matt. 25:10). And the church is referred to as his bride (Rev. 18:23; 21:2-9; 22:17). In 2 Corinthians 11:2 Paul speaks of betrothing the church as "a pure virgin to Christ." False teachers were attempting to woo the church away from Christ. Paul, who had done so much to nurture the church, and had founded the Corinthian congregation, spoke of his jealousy for her. He wanted to present her as a pure bride to Christ.

In The Revelation John speaks of the "marriage supper of the lamb" that will take place when Christ returns (Rev. 19:7-9). The idea is that we are engaged to Christ now, and the marriage will be consummated at his second coming. We will enter into the full and final union with him at that time.

And in Ephesians 5:21-33 Paul uses the relationship between Christ and his church as a great model of the relationship that should exist between a husband and his wife. Wives are to submit to their husbands as unto the Lord because the husband is head of the wife "as Christ is the head of the church." And husbands are to love their wives as Christ loved the church and gave himself for it. Though he does not use the words, Paul clearly pictures Christ as a husband and the church as his bride.

So, throughout scripture the Lord is referred to as the bridegroom and his people, the church, are called his bride. What does it mean, in practical terms, to say that the church is the bride of Christ? For one thing, it tells us something about Christ. He is the lover of humanity who has come to woo and win us to himself. But, more than that, it tells us something about ourselves. He has chosen us and we have accepted his proposal by saying "yes" to him. We now belong to him. We are his and we have committed ourselves to a loving, joyous, intimate, and faithful relationship with him.

This metaphor tells us some significant things about the church. As his bride we are to be marked by four things.

- We are to have a love for Christ.
- We are to have joy in Christ.
- We are to have intimacy with Christ.
- We are to have fidelity to Christ.

My Jesus, I Love Thee

First, as his bride, we are to have a love for Christ. The most characteristic thing about a bride is her deep, abiding love for her husband. To be sure, marriage involves commitment, but this commitment has its roots in love. If we are the bride of Christ, the single most characteristic thing about us ought to be our love for Christ.

Most of us readily identify with Simon Peter. That's because he seemed always to be saying or doing the wrong thing. But, despite his many mistakes, there was no doubt he loved the Lord. Even on the night of his denial, when the Lord looked at him, he went out and wept bitterly. No Pharisee ever did that.

When he met the Lord by the Sea of Galilee, the

Lord's one question was, "Simon, son of Jonah, do you love me?" The Lord didn't ask, "Simon, do you love being an apostle? Or, Simon do you love shepherding sheep? Or even, Simon, do you love sheep?" His question was, "Simon, do you love *me*?" That is the crucial issue. That is the thing that distinguishes us as his followers.

In his last word to the church, the risen Christ rebuked the church at Ephesus because they had left their first love (Rev. 2:1-5). Once a caring, compassionate people, they had lost their original drive for and devotion to Christ.

There were many good things the Lord had to say about this church. They were diligent in their works, orthodox in their beliefs, and patient in their endurance. But, none of these things could substitute for loving the Lord with all their heart and mind and soul.

So, to be the bride of Christ means first and foremost that we have a love for him. This love is the foundation of the church. What brings us together as a church? It is not because we like one another. Some church members aren't easy to like. The meanest man I know was in church every Sunday. He never missed a service.

Nor is it our burden for the lost or our great social concerns. To be sure, we do often like one another and we do have a burden for the lost and we do have a social concern. But all of these grow out of our love for Christ. We like one another because his love has been shed abroad in our hearts. We are burdened for the lost because he places a burden on us. And we have social concerns because he said "inasmuch as you have done it unto one of the least of these my brethren you have done it unto me."

Christ is the center and the circumference of our faith. If we reduced our faith to its lowest common denominator, it would come to one word: J-E-S-U-S. He is the one before whom we bow, through whom we pray, with whom we walk, to whom we look, and in whom we live and move and have our being.

Who is this Jesus whom we love? He is the lamb of God who takes away the sins of the world. He is the bread of life who satisfies the deepest hunger of our souls. He is the good shepherd who leads us through the valley of the shadow of death. He is the great physician who heals all of our hurts. He is the door through which we enter into the presence of God. He is the high priest who ever lives to make intercessions for us. He is the first fruits of them that slept. He is the Alpha and the Omega and all the letters of the alphabet in between. He is the king of kings and the lord of lords.

We always express our deepest feelings in music, so we sing:

Jesus, Jesus, Jesus
There's just something about that name,
Master, Savior, Jesus,
Like the fragrance after the rain;

Jesus, Jesus, Jesus,
Let all heaven and earth proclaim,
Kings and kingdoms shall all pass away,
But there's something about that name.

and

> *Jesus is the sweetest name I know,*
> *And he's just the same as his lovely name,*
> *And that's the reason why I love him so;*
> *Oh, Jesus is the sweetest name I know.*

and

> *My Jesus, I love thee, I know thou art mine,*
> *For thee all the follies of sin I resign;*
> *My gracious redeemer, my Savior art thou;*
> *If ever I loved thee, my Jesus, 'tis now.*

As his bride, the prayer of all of us ought to be, "Lord, help me to see thee more clearly, follow thee more nearly, and love thee more dearly."

Wedding Guests, Not Pallbearers

Next, as the bride of Christ we are to have joy in Christ. A shining, radiant joy is the second most obvious characteristic of a bride. She is happy and you can not only see it on her face, she wants to tell everyone about her new husband. If we, then, are the bride of Christ, we ought to find our joy in him also.

The Pharisees once asked Jesus why his disciples did not fast as John the Baptist's disciples did. Jesus answered them, "Can the children of the bride chamber (members of the wedding party) mourn, as long as the bridegroom is with them?" (Matt. 9:15).

Fasting was a grim, austere practice. It was like being on a perpetual diet. Christ's movement was not to be anything like that. His kingdom, he said, is to be characterized by feasting, not fasting. It is to be more like a wedding than a wake. And his followers are to look and act more like groomsmen than pallbearers. Jesus expected and still expects his disciples to be immensely happy.

The missing note of many churches and many Christians' lives today is that of joy. Mother Teresa, the Albanian nun who planted her life among the poor of Calcutta, India, was once asked about the qualifications for people who serve with her. She responded, "They must have the ability to learn, the capacity to know Jesus, and be ready to serve him — joyfully, not grumbling and not dragging their feet."

There should be no grumbling, no dragging the feet in God's service anywhere. As the Coptic Christian said, "If you carry the cross on your shoulder, you should do it without complaint."

Why shouldn't it be that way? We are the bride of Christ and serving him should be a joy. Samuel Shoemaker was right, "The surest mark of a Christian is not faith, or even love, but joy."

They Two Shall Become One Flesh

Third, as the bride of Christ we ought to have an intimacy with him. Marriage is the most intimate of all human relationships. The scriptures say, "Therefore shall a man leave his father and his mother, and shall cleave (be glued) unto his wife: and they shall be one flesh" (Gen. 2:24). The "one flesh" phrase refers to the sexual union in marriage. So intimate is this sexual union between a man and woman that the Bible speaks of it as to "know" another person. It describes the deepest, most intimate of all relationships.

If we then are the bride of Christ, we ought to have a deep, abiding relationship with him. An old bishop in India was approached by a missionary who asked, "Bishop, I have sought a deeper experience with God all these years. And I don't have it. I have read books about what to do, and I have kept all the rules, but I am nowhere yet. Does God have favorites?"

The wise old bishop replied, "No, my dear, God does not have favorites. But he does have intimates."

If you are a part of the bride of Christ, you ought to have an intimate relationship with him. By intimacy with Christ I'm not talking about some mystical experience, reserved for the spiritually elite. I'm not talking about some "deeper life." When it comes to the deeper life movement, I'm a lot like that country preacher who was invited to preach in a cultured church. He had no car so he rode the bus to get there. The deacon picked him up and asked, "Brother, do you preach the deeper things of the Bible?" "What do you mean?"

"Do you preach the deeper life?" "I'm not sure," said the preacher, "I preach on hell. Is that deep enough?"

A life of intimacy is the normal Christian life. It involves walking and talking with Christ and responding to him on a daily basis. It's to know him and to grow like him.

There is a vast difference in knowing about a person and knowing them. I knew about Donald Carter, former owner of the Dallas Mavericks professional basketball team, a long time. For years I watched his television ads for the Mavericks. The ads usually showed him standing up with his arm extended up and out above his head and his fist clenched as if to say, "Charge, Mavericks!" It seldom affected the team, but it was a good ad.

Then one night I had dinner with the Carters. His wife, Linda, and I served together on the board of trustees of Baylor University. And now we serve together on the board of Baylor Medical Center in Dallas. So we have dined together on several occasions.

Don is one of the most exuberant, effervescent, enthusiastic people I have ever known. And if you are around him much, his spirit rubs off on you.

That's what I mean by being intimate with Jesus. I mean you get to know him in such a way that he "rubs off" on you. Do you walk with him? Talk with him? Enjoy him? Has he rubbed off on you?

That is our joy and our privilege as the bride of Christ.

Stay Out of Bed with Other Lovers

Fourth, as the bride of Christ we are to have a fidelity to him. Fidelity is the cornerstone of marriage. Without faithfulness to your spouse, marriage in the strictest sense cannot be. The scriptures say, "Marriage is honorable in all, and the bed undefiled: but whoremongers and adulterers God will judge" (Heb. 13:4).

No marriage can last without fidelity and, as his bride, we must be as faithful to him as he is to us.

Sports Illustrated (March 6, 1989, pages 47-53) carried a story about Steve Garvey, former star first baseman of the Los Angeles Dodgers and later with the San Diego Padres. The article pointed out that for two decades sportswriters strained for ways to describe Steve Garvey. He had the image of being squeaky clean, the boy next door — wholesome and handsome, a role model for our youth.

He had married his college sweetheart and by her had two children. After ten years, their marriage ended and Garvey began to date other women. Then he married again. But, as he married, he was threatened with paternity suits by two other women with whom he reportedly had affairs during the past year. In public interviews he admitted that he might be the father of these two children, and if it could be established medically that these were his children then he would support both of them because he was, as he said, a Christian and he lived by Christian principles.

As a result of his claims on one hand and his conduct on the other, Garvey became the butt of many jokes. A San Diego radio station is gave out T-shirts that said, "I got to first base with Steve Garvey." And in Boston a new bumper sticker appeared, "Honk if you are carrying Steve Garvey's baby."

The unbelieving world delights to mock the name of Christ when his bride is not faithful to him. Listen, if you are the bride of Christ, stay out of bed with other gods. You belong to him exclusively. You are not to chase other lovers. You are to be true to him.

There are many wonderful organizations and movements that deserve your time, your influence, and your money. But none of them are to usurp the place of Christ in your life. He is your first love and he deserves your devotion and fidelity.

I have many lady friends. I laugh with them, talk with them, and enjoy their friendship. But I do not go to bed with them. I am faithful to my wife. Just so, as a Christian you can be a part of many organizations. You can give them your time, influence, and your money. But remember your first allegiance is to Christ. You owe him absolute fidelity.

The late Huber Drumwright was dean of the School of Theology at Southwestern Baptist Theological Seminary and later executive secretary of the Arkansas Baptist Convention. He once told that when he was a student in the seminary and having a hard time financially, he went to a bank in his hometown of Dallas to borrow some money. He gathered all the collateral he had, sat down with a loan officer, and told him he needed to borrow $500. His banker immediately said he would loan him the money. Dr. Drumwright was shocked. He said, "Don't I need any collateral?" The banker replied, "No! I've been a member of the First Baptist Church of Dallas for the past twenty years and my Sunday School teacher has been Huber Drumwright, Sr. Anybody who bears his name is good with me."

Every person has three names. The one they are born with, the one they make for themselves by the way they live, the things they do, and the one they take upon themselves. In marriage a woman takes upon herself the name of her husband. And, in commitment to Christ we take upon ourselves his name.

As the bride of Christ, we bear his name. And, to have his name ought to be good with anybody, anywhere, anytime.

Chapter 3

The Church, His Body

Colossians 1:18

Dr. W. R. Pettigrew, longtime pastor in Louisville, Kentucky, told of a little crippled boy whose only means of making a living was selling notions in the lobby of a train station. He sat all day on a high stool with a large tray, and sold to the travelers who came by. One day a man rushed to catch a train, whirled around the corner, and crashed into the little boy before he saw him. The stool went one way, the boy another, and the trinkets scattered all over the floor. Instead of apologizing, the irate man gave the boy a dirty stare, muttered under his breath, and stalked over to catch the train.

Another traveler was rushing to catch the same train, but saw what had happened, set down his bag, put the stool back on its feet, helped the little boy back upon it, and stooped down and gathered up the trinkets off of the floor. Then he reached in his pocket, pulled out ten dollars, and gave it to the boy saying, "Here, this will pay for the notions that got lost and broken."

The man then picked up his bag and turned to leave, but he was stopped dead in his tracks by the sound of the little boy's voice. He called out, "Wait, Mister, wait, wait, Mister, are you Jesus?" The man turned around and said, "No, son. I'm not Jesus; but I am one of his followers who is trying to do what he would do if he were here."

I submit to you that this is the church in action — the church as it ought to be — acting and serving in ways that make people see Jesus in what is done. The Bible says we are the body of Christ. That means that we are to do on earth what Jesus would do if he were here physically. The apostle Paul declares of the risen Christ, "And he is the head of the body, the church . . ." (Col. 1:18). This is the most common analogy for the church in the Bible. It is used fifteen times in the New Testament.

What do the scriptures mean when they refer to the church as the body of Christ? For 33 years Jesus was God incarnated in a human body. Through that body he went about doing good. With his eyes he saw the hurts of those around him, with his ears he heard the cries of the oppressed. With his feet he went to their side. With his hands he healed them and fed them. With his voice he spoke God's word to them.

In time he died on the old rugged cross, was buried in Joseph's tomb, arose from the dead on the third day and ascended into heaven. Then on the day of Pentecost the Holy Spirit, the living spirit of Christ, came back to earth to dwell in his people and to constitute his church. So, while God was incarnated as Jesus in a body for 33 years, he now perpetually incarnates himself in his new body, the church.

We are now his body on earth. What that suggests, in part, is we are the means through which Christ expresses his personality and by which he ministers. We are his hands, his feet, his voice here on earth. The world does not see Christ unless it sees him in and through us. What his physical body was to the incarnate Christ, the church is to the risen Christ.

What, then, are we to do as his body on earth today? What is our responsibility, our mission on earth? To answer those questions we need only look at Jesus and see what he did through his body when he was on earth. And that is what we are to do as his body today. What did Jesus do? He fed the hungry, clothed the naked, healed the sick, befriended sinners, preached the gospel, and eventually gave his very life for the world. In short, he put his body at the disposal of God for the service of humanity . . . seeing, listening, loving, touching, feeling, healing, and preaching.

That's what we are to do! We are not to see ourselves as spectators in the arena of life, but as servants. We are the hands of Christ to reach out to the needy; we are the eyes of Christ to see the hurt of human hearts; we are the ears of Christ to hear the cries of the distressed; we are the feet of Christ to rush to the side of the oppressed; we are the voice of Christ to speak his message of salvation and hope.

As his body he wants to live in us so that he can live through us. Through our hands he wants to reach out. Through our feet he wants to step out and through our eyes he wants to look out. Through our lips he wants to speak out. But if we are not available to him then no work is done for him.

He wants to be in you and in me what he was when he walked among men nineteen centuries ago. He was then the Son of God in power, and he wants to be that in us today. In principle, he wants to do in you, and through you, exactly what he did when he was here in the flesh in the first century.

The analogy of a body suggests several things we need to know about the church.

- We are to respond to Christ.
- We are to be unified in Christ.
- We are to minister for Christ.

Not a Tool of the Social Order

First, we are to respond to Christ. The Bible declares that Christ is the head of the church. We are members of the body and he is the head of the body. This means that Christ bears the same relationship to the church that my head bears to my body.

My head is the control center of my life. It is the location of my will. It is the seat of my decision making process. I do nothing with my body unless my brain first tells it to do so.

The movie, "Bound for Glory," the story of folk singer Woody Guthrie, tells about the depression era in Texas and the difficulties people went through. In one scene Woody was talking with a lady who had lost a child and was so deeply depressed she wouldn't eat. As he tried to help her he said, "Everyone knows the mind is the boss of the whole body. It tells the hands and the legs and the mouth and the throat and every other part of the body what to do."

Woody was right. If I reach out with my hand, it is because my mind sends an impulse through my nerves to my muscles and the hand responds. If I take a step, it is because my mind tells my foot to do so. If I speak a word, my mind first makes the decision and relays the message to my vocal cords. My body does nothing without my mind first telling it to. So my head makes the decisions and my body responds to carry out what the mind tells it to do.

In the same way Christ is to control, to direct the actions of the church. The church is here to carry out his will, to obey his commands, to do his work on earth. We, as his body, are to respond to his will, fulfill his desires, obey his dictates.

Babe Pinelli, the famed professional baseball umpire, once called Babe Ruth out on strikes in one of his games. The Babe gave an argument. He said, "There's 40,000 people here who know that last one was a ball, tomato head."

Pinelli responded with a calm voice and stately manner: "Maybe so, but mine is the only opinion that counts out here."

In the church, we need to know only one opinion matters — Christ's. He is the head of the church and we are to respond to him.

It is possible, however, for a person's mind to be sharp and clear, to function normally and his/her body not to function like it ought to. This can happen for a lot of different reasons.

The body can be paralyzed by an accident. General George S. Patton, who commanded the Third Army as it swept across Europe in the final days of World War II and clinched the victory for the Allied Forces, was involved in an automobile accident the day before he was to return to the United States and was paralyzed from the neck down. As the General lay in the hospital he could see, hear, speak, remember and think clearly. But he could not move a single part of his body from his neck down. He was completely paralyzed. Just so, it is possible for Christ, the head of the church, to be alive and well, but for his body, the church, to be paralyzed by fear or indifference.

A person's body can be weakened by disease. One day, years ago, I visited in the homes of two men in my congregation who were terminally ill. Both of them had once been robust, working men. But now they had cancer in advanced stages. The doctor had given them just a few weeks to live. As we talked, they both thought and spoke with perfect clarity. Their minds were as sharp and as clear as they had ever been. But their bodies were slowly wasting away through disease and they could no longer feed, bathe, or dress themselves. In the same way it is possible for Christ as the head of the church to be alive and well and his body, the church, to be weakened by strife and discord.

And one's body can waste away by inactivity and old age. There was a time when I had the body fat of a coat hanger. I was keen and lean and mean. I could run up and down a basketball court all day long. I could jump as high as the hoop. But nowadays I find myself sagging and dragging and lagging in almost everything I do. In fact, now, when I bend down to tie my shoe laces I look around to see if there is anything else I can do while I'm down there. Now, when I exercise vigorously, I hurt in places I used to not even know I had places. It is all a result of my body wasting away through age. My doctor tells me my problem is I have a "type A" personality in a "Model T" body.

My mind is okay, but my body simply does not respond as it used to. Just so, it is possible for Christ, the head, to be alive and well today and for his body, the church, to grow old in its spirit and attitude.

One of the great tragedies of Christendom is that the body of Christ is not healthy and vigorous as it ought to be. Christ, the head of the church, is alive and well on planet earth, but his body, his church, often does not respond to him as we ought. To be his body means we are to respond to him.

All I Can Do Is Make Money

Second, we are to be united in Christ. In all of these analogies of the church — a bride, a building, the family, an army and a body — "togetherness" is the key.

Soldiers together make an army. A bride and a groom together make a marriage. Relatives together make a family. And bricks together make a building. Parts together make a body. And people together, united in Christ, make a church.

One soldier does not make an army, one person does not make a marriage, one relative does not make a family, one brick does not make a building and one member does not make a body. So the church of Jesus Christ must have a togetherness about it to be a body.

Several times the apostle Paul uses the analogy of the human body to teach us about the unity and diversity of the church. Our bodies are made up of many parts — hands, feet, eyes, etc. Each part is different. They were created to perform different functions. I see with my eyes, I hear with my ears, I touch with my hands, I walk with my feet. I have had people say, "Keep talking, I'm all ears." But aren't you glad we aren't all ears? How would we see? or walk? or talk if we were all ears? And I have heard people say, "I'm all thumbs." Aren't you glad we aren't all thumbs? How would we grip things? or smell?

And while each part is different, each part is also important. There are no useless parts to my body. I can live without some parts of my body, i.e., my tonsils, my appendix, but they are important nonetheless. Now these various parts are not equally prominent or equally attractive, i.e., my toe is not as prominent as my nose or my ribs as noticeable as my eyes, but they are all important. And each has a vital function to perform.

The various parts of my body, while different, all work in harmony with one another. With my hands I pick up my food. With my teeth I chew it. With my stomach I digest it. There is no competition between the parts. They all work together to meet my every need. Each part is different, each part is vital, and each part is cooperative. They are not jealous or envious of one another.

Just so, the church, Christ's body, is made up of many members. Each one has been given spiritual gifts to be used for the good of the whole body. And, as with the human body, each member is important. There are no useless parts in the body of Christ. Just as with the human body, some parts are more visible, more prominent than others. But they are all vital.

The apostle Paul lists some of these gifts in Rom. 12:6-8. They are the gifts of prophecy (preaching), the gift of ministry (helping people in need), the gift of teaching, the gift of exhortation (the ability to inspire and encourage others), the gift of giving (which implies the ability to make money), the gift of ruling (the ability to lead), and the gift of mercy (a sympathetic heart to reach out and comfort people).

The value of visiting the elderly in a nursing home is not as visible as singing in the choir, but it is just as important. And the importance of chairing a committee is not as prominent as preaching to 1,000 people or teaching a Sunday School class of children, but it is just as valuable. Some are "out front" functions and some are "behind the scenes" functions, but they are all vital to a healthy church body.

Paul wrote what he did about these gifts because they had become a source of strife in the church. Some members were jealous of other members because they did not have gifts that were as spectacular as some others. And, some were puffed up with pride because they felt they were superior to others who had less noticeable gifts. Paul chided these Christians, saying there should be no competition in the church (1 Cor. 12:25). The gifts are all given by God's grace and are not to divide us, but to unite us. They should be received and administered not in arrogance or pride, but in humility and in harmony.

When that is the case the body functions as a whole and every need is met.

In practical terms this means each of us needs to find his/her place in the body and fill it. We need to discover what our gift is, develop it to its highest potential, and then dedicate it to the Lord.

In San Angelo, Texas, years ago I met a wonderful Christian layman named Melvin Shook. Early in his life, with $300 and the signature of two friends on a note, he bought a tire company. It eventually grew to the largest tire distributorship in all of west Texas.

During the depression years Mr. Shook personally supported the entire mission work of the Foreign Mission Board of the Southern Baptist Convention in the Amazon Valley of Brazil. Through the years he has given untold millions to missions and to educate Christian young people.

When Dr. Jerold McBride went to the church as pastor, Mr. Shook said to him, "Preacher, I am a one-talented man. I can't do anything but make money. But, my money belongs to God. So, if you know of some need I can meet, feel free to ask me. If you won't be offended if I say no, I won't be offended if you ask me."

Though he is a multimillionaire, Mr. Shook drives a medium priced car. For years his pastor encouraged him to buy a more luxurious one. But he always refused saying, "Preacher, I just couldn't do that. This is not my money. It is God's money. A more expensive car would cost me at least $5,000 more than the kind I drive, and I can always see some place that needs the $5,000 more than I need a more expensive car."

Mr. Shook could never teach a Sunday School class, or sing in the choir, or do a lot of things in the church, but God has given him a gift of making and giving money and he is exercising that gift faithfully. There are others in the church who can't give millions, but they can sing and teach. If each person does what he/she can, all the needs of the body are met. That's what it means to be the body of Christ — we are not only to respond to Christ, we harmonize in Christ.

He Has No Hands But Our Hands

Third, we are to minister for Christ. We are to be his servants on earth. This, I believe, is what W. O. Carver meant when he said, "The church is an extension of the incarnation."

In the courtyard of a quaint little church in a French village there stood a beautiful statue of Jesus with his hands outstretched. One day during World War II a bomb struck too close to the statue and it was dismembered. After the battle was over the citizens of the village decided to find the pieces of their beloved statue and reconstruct it. Patiently they gathered the broken pieces and reassembled it. Even the scars on the body added to its beauty. But there was one problem. They were unable to find the hands of the statue. "A Christ without hands is no Christ at all," someone lamented. "Hands with scars, yes. But what's a Lord without hands? We need a new statue." Then someone else came along with another idea and it prevailed. A brass plaque was attached to the base of the statue which read, "I have no hands, but your hands."

Years later someone saw the inscription and wrote these lines:

Christ has no hands but our hands
To do his work today;
He has no feet but our feet
To lead men in his way.
He has no tongue but our tongues,
To tell men how he died.
He has no help but our help,
To bring men to his side.

We are the only Bible,
The careless world will read.
We are the sinner's gospel,
We are the scoffer's creed;
We are the Lord's last message,
Written indeed in word —
What if the line be crooked?
What if the type be blurred.

Our ministry for Christ is to extend in two directions. First, we are to minister to one another. When my leg itches, my hand automatically reaches down to scratch it and make it feel better. When I hit my thumb with a hammer, I instinctively put it in my mouth to soothe it. One part of my body ministers to the other parts when they hurt. That's the way it is to be with the church, his body. Paul says, "And whether one member suffer, all the members suffer with it; or one member be honored, all the members rejoice with it" (1 Cor. 12:26).

But we don't spend all our time on ourselves. We are also to minister to the world. I don't spend all my time rubbing and petting on myself. And I don't go around sucking my thumb all the time. I also reach out to help other people. As his body we are Christ's hands and as he reached out to minister to others, we are to reach out and minister to others also.

That's what it means to be the body of Christ. It means we are to respond to him . . . we are to be united in him . . . and we are to minister for him. One other thing — the parts of the body are of no value unless they are attached. These hands of mine have been perfectly good hands all of my life, but if I cut them off from the rest of the body they will cease to be useful. Just so, a Christian unattached to the body is useless in the kingdom of God. Every believer needs to be attached to the body and functioning in accordance with the gift God has given him/her.

Today, through the wonder of medicine, many parts of the body that have been severed can be sewed back and made to function normally. If you have been severed by sin from the body of Christ, the great physician can restore you if you will let him.

Chapter 4

The Church, His Family

1 Timothy 3:14-15

In a dispatch written after one of his great naval victories, Lord Nelson ascribed his victory to the fact that he had the "happy privilege to command a band of brothers." Unless the church is a band of brothers (and sisters) it is not a church at all. The love of God can only exist where brotherly love exists.

This idea of the church as a brotherhood, as a family, is used often in scripture. The words used in the New Testament most frequently for Christians are brother or sister or child of God.

One place where this analogy of a family is used is where the apostle Paul spoke of the church as "the house of God, which is the church of the living God, the pillar and ground of truth" (1 Tim. 3:15).

The apostle hoped to visit Timothy, but fearing he may be delayed, wrote this letter of instruction concerning the management of affairs in the church. He wanted Timothy to be a worthy minister and encouraged him in his pastoral duties. As he does he describes the church as the "house of God." The phrase literally means "the household" or "the family" of God.

What does Paul mean by the use of this analogy? The idea of a family suggests that a church is supposed to be a caring and sharing fellowship. It is to be a loving and accepting family where people who have been born again can be nurtured to full maturity in Christ.

The church is not a building, although it meets in one. The church is not an organization, although it may be organized. And the church is not an audience, although it may comprise one from time to time. The church is the living family of the living God.

It is as simple as this, if God is your father and God is my father, then we are brothers and sisters in Christ. We are a family. I am old enough to recall the days when we used to refer to one another as Brother and Sister in the church. I'm not pleading that we reclaim that terminology, but I do wish we could reclaim that spirit of family that we once knew.

Every association of persons has some central unifying element. The church did not arise simply through people having feelings for one another or because they agree on the issues of life. The central unifying element of the church is our common commitment to God as father through faith in Jesus Christ. There is absolutely no sense in talking about the brotherhood of man without first talking about the fatherhood of God. And there is no need to talk about knowing God without first talking about faith in Jesus Christ (John 14:6).

The horizontal relationship of life is always derivative, not primary; the vertical must come first and then, after the vertical, comes the horizontal fellowship with one another.

We are not frozen together by formality; we are not rusted together by tradition; and we are not wired together by organization. We are cemented together by a common commitment to God as Father through faith in the son Jesus Christ.

The Bible knows nothing of a solitary religion. If you take God as your father, you take the church as your family. God does not want his children to be nomads, hermits, or recluses. He wants us to live in fellowship with him and with one another.

To say that the church is a family is to say it is the closest, warmest kind of fellowship. More than any service club, more than any fraternal order, more than any sorority, more than any political party, more than any professional organization.

Through the new birth we are born again and thus enter into God's family. We are, then, brothers and sisters in Christ. So the church is for us what a good family is for its members.

If the church is a family, what kind of place ought it to be?

- The church ought to be a place of gladness.
- The church ought to be a place of growth.
- The church ought to be a place of grace.

Like a Family Reunion

First, if the church is a family it ought to be a place of gladness. If you were to ask me, "What is the single most important characteristic of a good home?" I would answer, "Happiness." The home ought, above all else, to be a place where people like to go and want to be. And if it is that, it has to be a happy place.

I realize that the home must be a place of discipline, but discipline makes for happiness. The home must be a place of responsibility, but responsibility is necessary to happiness. The home must be a place of respect, but respect is essential to happiness. The home must be a place of love, but loving and being loved is inherent in happiness. The home must be a place of caring, but caring people are happy people. So, if a home is a happy place it must of necessity be a place of discipline, responsibility, respect, love, and caring.

If, then, the church is the family of God, it also ought to be a place of laughter, a place of joy, a place where people like to go and want to be. But, that often is not the case. In many churches the preacher talks in a trembling voice that makes you feel the heavens are going to fall; the choir sings at such a slow tempo that the music sounds like a funeral dirge; and the members are often cold and unfriendly.

A young man told me recently he had visited a church for an entire year and not one person spoke to him. Four times he filled out visitor's cards and not once did the minister, a staff person, or a member of the congregation call him, write him, or visit him. Can a home be a happy place when guests are not welcome or where people don't speak to one another?

Still, other churches are places of conflict and strife. The members are constantly squabbling. Who wants to be a part of a bickering, arguing, complaining family? Do you remember the story of the three bears? Mama Bear prepared the porridge for dinner and she called Papa Bear and Baby Bear to the table. When Papa Bear bowed his head to say grace he looked into an empty bowl and said, "Somebody has been eating my porridge, and they've eaten it all up." Baby Bear looked down and he said, "Somebody's been eating my porridge, and they've eaten it all up." And Mama Bear said, "Shut up your yak-yak. I haven't poured the porridge yet."

Some churches have entirely too much yak-yak. That's out of place in the family of God. We can disagree without being disagreeable. We can share convictions without becoming argumentative. If we are the family of God, we need to be a happy, harmonious people.

The most important quality of a growing church is a spirit of love and joy that embraces everyone who walks through the doors. There are no walls or false faces, the people are eager to bear one another's burdens. The pastor's love for the people is expressed, accepted, and returned. It is a happy place.

The psalmist said, "I was glad when they said unto me, let us go into the house of the Lord" (Ps. 122:1). Unless people are saying that about their church it is not like a family and it will not grow as it should.

God's "One Another" Plan

Second, if the church is a family it should be a place of growth. The purpose of the church is not just mutual enjoyment, but also for mutual enrichment for spiritual development. It is to be a place where we can grow to our full potential in Christ.

A favorite pastime of sinners outside the church is to call the sinners inside the church hypocrites. The word "hypocrite" originated in the field of drama in the days when one person played several parts in a play. The performer wore a different mask for each character portrayed. In one scene he might be the villain. In the next he might be the hero. He simply put on a different mask for each character. Such a person was called a hypocrite. The word had a good meaning at first, but gradually it came to describe a person who was two-faced, one who was play-acting or pretending religiosity.

I am sure there are hypocrites in the church. Billy Sunday said, "You can find anything in the average church today from a hummingbird to a turkey buzzard." I'm sure he was right. But not all who fail to live up to their profession of faith are hypocrites. Many are just weak and immature Christians. Critics fail to realize that in a large and growing family, there are people at various ages and stages of maturity. There may be parents, who are adults, teenagers, or adolescents, and even children or infants. No one expects everyone in that kind of family to act alike. Infants don't act like children, children don't act like teenagers, teenagers don't act like adults. The fact is, a part of the purpose of a family is to help each person grow from his/her present level of maturity to his/her full potential.

The church, as a family of God, is the same way. In the church there are different levels of maturity. Some have just been born again. They are infants in the faith. Others are spiritual adolescents. And others are mature spiritually.

The oldest active member of the last congregation I pastored was 96 years of age. At that age he was still singing in the choir. He had to be helped up the steps into the choir loft. And when he stood he leaned against the wall to keep from falling over. It gave new meaning to the old hymn, "Leaning on the Everlasting Arms."

He became a Christian at the age of ten. That means he had been a Christian for 86 years. But there were some in the congregation who had not been Christians 86 days. They had not yet learned how to walk and talk and act as Christians. They needed time to grow in their faith. In the church, just as in a family, we don't expect the same kind of behavior from everyone. And, if I understand what a church family is all about, it is to be a place where people are accepted at whatever level of maturity they are and helped and encouraged to grow to full maturity in Christ.

The church has been called by some a "mothering community." It is a place where people are loved, accepted, helped, and encouraged as they grow. It is a place where each member takes upon himself the responsibility for the spiritual life of the other members of the church. Every member is to help every other member to be a better Christian. It is a place where all newborn Christians can gather in fellowship and worship and service and receive the nourishment, understanding, and guidance that makes growth possible. The church is to grow not just by addition, but also by nutrition.

The writer of the book of Hebrews puts it this way, "Let us consider one another to provoke unto love and to good works: not forsaking the assembling of ourselves together, as the manner of some is; but exhorting one another: and so much the more, as we see the day approaching" (Heb. 10:24-25).

I want you to note the words "one another" in that verse. God has a long list of "one anothers" that must not be ignored if the church is to shine forth as a beacon in the world. The spiritual candle power of individual Christians will become brighter as more of God's "one anothers" plan works in us.

We are to "love one another" (John 13:34-35); We are to "depend on one another" (Rom. 12:5); We are to "be devoted to one another" (Rom. 12:10); We are to "honor one another" (Rom. 12:10); We are to "rejoice with one another" (Rom. 12:15; 1 Cor. 12:26); We are to "weep with one another" (Rom. 12:15); We are to "be of the same mind toward one another" (Rom. 12:16); We are "not to judge one another" (Rom. 14:13); We are to "accept one another" (Rom. 15:7); We are to "admonish one another" (Rom. 15:14); We are to "salute one another" (Rom. 16:16); We are to "wait for one another" (1 Cor. 11:33); We are to "care for one another" (1 Cor. 12:25); We are to "serve one another" (Gal. 5:13); We are to "be kind one to another" (Eph. 4:32); We are to "forgive one another" (Eph. 4:32; Col. 3:13); We are to "be tenderhearted toward one another" (Eph. 4:32); We are to "encourage one another" (1 Thes. 5:11); We are to "submit to one another" (Eph. 5:21); We are to "forbear (uphold) one another" (Eph. 4:2; Col. 3:13); We are to "provoke (stimulate) one another" (Heb. 10:24); We are to "show hospitality one to another" (1 Peter 4:9); We are to "minister gifts one to another" (1 Peter 4:10); We are to "be humble one toward another" (1 Peter 5:5); We are "not to speak evil against one another" (James 4:11); We are "not to grumble against one another" (James 5:9); We are to "confess our faults one to another" (James 5:16); We are to "pray one for another" (James 5:16); We are to "fellowship with one another" (1 John 1:7); We are "not to be puffed up against one another" (1 Cor. 4:6); We are "to bear one another's burdens" (Gal. 6:2).

If the "one another" plan of God is put to practice we will be a family in the fullest sense of the word. It will ensure that no single member will ever have to struggle alone in the battles of life.

We realize that none of us is a perfect person. We are under no illusions about our sin. So we are patient; we are to be gentle; we are forgiving; we are long-suffering; we are to be forbearing with one another as we strive to become our best for him.

The African proverb says, "It takes the whole village to raise a child." In the same way it takes the whole church to help a new Christian reach maturity in Christ.

Throwing Ropes, Not Rocks

Third, if the church is a family it must be a place of grace. Robert Frost once wrote:

"Home is the place where, when you go there,
They have to take you in.
I should have called it,
Something you haven't to deserve."

Whatever else the home is, it is a place of grace. You don't have to merit or earn your place in it. It is yours by birth.

I think I learned more about grace by being a parent than any other way. In my family we have three children. Two boys and a girl. They are all grown and gone. Thank the Lord! Those two boys of mine, I believe, were out to prove that everything ever said about the preacher's kid was an understatement.

Anybody who raises teenagers in today's world should have no fear of the tribulation. For my wife and me it would have been a welcome relief.

At times, as our family grew, there were tears, disappointments, frustrations, anger, embarrassment, and shame. But I want you to know, through it all, they were still my family. And I never quit loving them, encouraging them, and praying for them. We stuck together. We didn't disown one another, reject one another, kick one another out. And our children always knew they had a home. I think that's a part of what family is all about.

And if the church is a family it will be the same way. It is a place, "you haven't deserved." It will be a place of hope, healing, and affirmation; a family in which everyone feels he belongs without worrying if there is some taint about him. Through Jesus there is a place for everyone of us in the family of God. Men may put up barriers but Jesus never does. The last great invitation in the book of Revelation is an invitation to all to come and be a part: "And the Spirit and the bride (church) say, come. And let him that heareth say, come. And let him that is athirst come. And whosoever will, let him take the water of life freely" (Rev. 22:17).

What the Lord says, we say. There is full and free acceptance in him . . . and there should be with us.

Kenneth Chafin, retired professor of evangelism at The Southern Baptist Theological Seminary, tells of a time when he taught 1 Corinthians to a group at Gulf Shore Baptist Assembly near Gulfport, Mississippi. As they discussed the fellowship of the church he asked, "If you really got into trouble, if your boy was in jail or your teenage daughter was pregnant, who would you most like to know about it?"

A sadness came over the room. Finally, one person spoke for all, and said, "I don't know who I'd like to know first, but I know who I would like to know last. I'd like for the people of my church to be the last to find out."

Sometimes the most critical, caustic, judgmental people on earth are in the church. Instead of being like a family that accepts, supports, and cares for people in trouble, we add to their troubles. As someone has said, "The Christian army is the only army that shoots its own wounded."

Some time ago a lady I know who was dying of cancer

called her nephew to her side. He had gone away from his church and from God. (And, by the way, you can't go away from the church without going away from God.) She had a special relationship with him and wanted to say a final word to him. Her word was this, "Son, you hang on to your church, for when the chips are down, it will hang on to you."

That's my word to you. Stay with the church because when the chips are down it will stay with you. It is your spiritual family.

Eventually everything you hold dear will be stripped from you. It is only a matter of when. Your family, your marriage, your money, your children, your friends — we all die or else they die. That is, all except your relationship to God. That is a possession, a reality, that nothing can touch. And, right next to that, is the church: his family.

Chapter 5

The Church, His Army

Matthew 16:18

E. O. Wyley, a retired professor from Southwest Texas State University in San Marcos, said to me when I was his pastor, "Paul, if we keep working at it, eventually we may make the First Baptist Church a Christian institution." The fact is, the church is always becoming. It is never quite all it ought to be.

What is the church to be? It is to be a loving bride, a serving body, a nurturing family, and it is to be a marching army.

The analogy of Christians as soldiers and the church as an army is common in the New Testament. Paul refers to Archippus and Epaphroditus as "fellow soldiers." And he encouraged Timothy to "Endure hardness as a good soldier of Jesus Christ" (2 Tim. 2:3).

The idea of the church as an army was first expressed by Jesus when he said, ". . . upon this rock I will build my church and the gates of hell shall not prevail against it" (Matt. 16:18).

Ancient cities were built with walls around them. Interspersed in the walls were gates. The purpose of the gates was not to keep the people in but to keep the enemy out. When attacked, the best means of defense for a city was to entrench itself behind its walls. The weakest place in the defense system was the gates, and it was there that the onslaught was made; it was there that the army tried to break through. So when Jesus said, "The gates of hell shall not prevail" against the church he was not picturing the defensive strength of the church, but rather the offensive strategy of the church.

With this statement Jesus was saying, "My church is to be like a mighty army, aggressively driving back the boundaries of darkness as it extends the kingdom of God to all persons everywhere." It was to be a bride in combat boots.

But, unfortunately, today the church is in retreat. Most churches seem satisfied to hold their own, or worse, they are being pushed around and beaten back. They are slipping backwards instead of surging forward. One leader expressed the decline this way: "Our sickness is like leukemia. We are wasting away."

Several years ago there was a movement to remove from the hymnal all militant hymns. Its proponents felt we should not sing such great hymns as:

Onward Christian soldiers, marching as to war,
With the cross of Jesus going on before!
Christ, the royal Master leads against the foe;
Forward into battle, see his banners go!

or, again,

> *Stand up, stand up for Jesus, ye soldiers of the cross;*
> *Lift high his royal banner, it must not suffer loss:*
> *From vict'ry unto vict'ry, his army shall he lead,*
> *Till ev'ry foe is vanquished, and Christ is Lord indeed.*

Their reason? They said these militant hymns were inappropriate in a Christian hymnal because they were an endorsement of war. I think another reason must be that, by-and-large, churches have lost their militant spirit.

The church today needs not only to keep its militant hymns, it needs also to recover a militant spirit. It needs to see itself as a bride — loving Christ; as a body — serving Christ; as a family — nurturing in Christ . . . and as an army — marching, advancing, conquering for Christ.

Like never before we need to ask ourselves, "What are the essentials of a spiritual offensive? How can the church take hold again like that, move in and not out, take some new territory, not surrender or just hold what we have?"

What do we need to do to make the church like a mighty army? I have put down four things:

- We must have an aggressive mind.
- We must have a global strategy.
- We must have a disciplined membership.
- We must have adequate power.

Bodyguards of the Status Quo

First, for the church to be like an army, it must have an aggressive mind. An aggressive mind is a mind alert to opportunity, quick to seize the initiative. That is essential for any army.

The most tragic war in American history was the Civil War fought 1861-1865. In that war we lost more American lives than in all other wars put together. While accurate casualty figures are almost impossible to obtain, as best we can tell, 744,342 men were killed. By comparison we lost 116,500 in World War I; 405,400 in World War II; 54,246 in the Korean War; 56,500 in the Vietnam War for a total of 632,646. Far short of the casualties of the great Civil War. The percentage of the population was even more staggering.

The Civil War not only divided the country, it also divided families so that brother fought against brother. The four years of bloodshed left a heritage of grief and bitterness that remains in part even today.

One of the tragedies of the Civil War is that it lasted far longer than it had to. The Union forces were far larger than those of the Confederacy. In the last year of the war the North had more than one million men in arms. The South probably had no more than 200,000. But the Union army had a succession of inept generals — George B. McClellan, Ambrose E. Burnside, Joseph Hooker, and George G. Mead. They all had one serious weakness — none of them were aggressive enough. It was not until Lincoln turned to the hard-driving, hard-drinking, cigar chewing Ulysses S. Grant that the balance swung to the north and the Confederacy was defeated.

On one occasion, as he looked over the Union troops, Lincoln said to one of his aides, "Look at that, Bro. Washburn, as far as the eye can see, do you know what that is?" Washburn replied, "The army of the Potomac." Lincoln said,

"No, Bro. Washburn, it is General McClellan's bodyguard."

Lincoln then said of McClellan, "He is a superb organizer. He has good points but he can't fight."

"Won't fight," said Washburn.

On another occasion Lincoln said to William Seward, his Secretary of State, "We have you, Mr. Seward, a sad progression of generals — McClellan, Burnside, Hooker, and Mead. They all wait to be attacked. It is not their nature to attack first."

We need to ask ourselves, as Christ's army, "Are we, like McClellan's army, a bodyguard of the status quo? Is it our nature to attack? Or do we wait to be attacked first?"

Lloyd George, prime minister of Great Britain during World War I, said, "No army can march on a retreating mind." The church today must realize that it is at war. We are in a spiritual warfare for the souls of men and women. We must get on the offensive.

We need to learn from the method of training in the United States Army. Some attention is given to defense, but much more to offense. Therein is the real secret of America's signal success. Our troops went to Europe to drive the Germans out of France and Belgium. General Bundy sounded the note that won the war. On being ordered by a superior officer at Chateau-Thierry to retreat, he replied, "Retreat! We have just come. We came not to retreat, but to advance."

We must not be content to sit and soak and sour until the second coming. We must not have a retreating mind. We must act aggressively if we are to be the army we were intended to be.

Hand written: Great Commission

D-Day for the Church

The second essential for the church to be like an army is a global strategy. Our mission is clear. It is world conquest, world evangelization. But between us and the world is our nation. And between us and our nation is our state. And between us and our state is our city. That is where we must start. We must begin by developing a strategy to reach our city or our town, or our neighborhood, for Christ.

We need a comprehensive battle plan, a far-sighted, imaginative strategy that involves the whole church preaching the whole gospel to the whole world. We must think globally and act locally.

In war, real war, every soldier has a job to do. Some are on the front lines doing battle, some are in communication, some are providing supplies, and some are at headquarters developing strategy. But everyone has a job to do — and they do it under the command of their leader. No army can hope to win a war with untrained, uncommitted, undisciplined troops, half of which are AWOL.

Rudyard Kipling expresses this truth in his *Barracks Room Ballads*. In one of the ballads he had one old soldier say, "It ain't the individual nor the army as a whole, but the everlasting teamwork of every bloomin' soul." In God's army every blooming person is important.

The largest church in the world is Central Gospel Church, in Seoul, Korea. It has a membership estimated at 500,000 and it is growing at a rate of 10,000 members a month. The pastor, Paul Y. Cho, has his city divided into 12 districts with numerous small cell groups in each district as his primary way of growth. Each cell is a homogenous group of not more than 15 families that meets once a week. They have a clear goal: it is the salvation of two souls a year — knowing that if they get two heads of households to accept Christ as Savior, their families will also become members of the family of God.

Pastor Cho said more than a decade ago, "On the wall of our church offices are maps and charts for each district. In fact, it looks like a military strategy room. This is war we are fighting. The enemy is the devil. The battlefield is the hearts of lost humanity. The object is to get as many souls saved as possible before Jesus comes." (Christianity Today, page 54, May 14, 1984.) That's the spirit we all need.

But do we have such a strategy? A global strategy? To know, all you need do is examine your dreams and plans. Little dreams and small goals betray us. Carl Bates, former president of the Southern Baptist Convention, once said, "There came a time in my life when I earnestly prayed, 'God, I want more power.' Time wore on and the power did not come. One day the burden was more than I could bear. I asked, 'God, why haven't you answered my prayer?' God seemed to whisper back his simple reply, 'With plans no bigger than yours, you don't need any power.'"

Ask yourself, is there one Sunday School class in your church that has a clear goal, understood by all in the class, that they will win two people to Christ this year? Is there a class that even has a goal of increasing their average attendance by two this year? Sadly, the goal of most classes is to meet next Sunday. Is there any wonder we are in retreat?

The early church was Christianity on the offensive. It had to make its way in a world much worse than ours. It sang its songs, said its prayers, and had in its mind a strategy for a larger offensive. It was after the impossible. In a matter of a few short years, it turned the first century world upside down. It did all of this without benefit of television, radio, the printed page, jet travel, or even buildings to meet in.

It is not too harsh a judgment to say that the average church today is neither vigorous, nor vocal, nor visual. The church today could silence its critics and restore its ministry by again having a membership filled with the Spirit of God and preaching and teaching everywhere. That must be our strategy until Jesus comes again.

Remember the Alamo

Third, for the church to be like an army it must have a disciplined membership. Most churches today are long on membership and short on discipleship. They appear to be more anxious about gathering statistics than growing saints. One minister, commenting on the low level of dedication in his denomination said, "The only requirement for confirmation is to have a heartbeat."

A veteran returned home from Vietnam and went to church one Sunday. He came home disgusted. His mother wanted to know why. He said, "We sang, 'Onward Christian Soldiers . . . marching as to war . . .' If we had marched together under our commander in Vietnam as Christians march under our commander, Jesus Christ, we'd have been driven into the sea." Is it any better with us?

It's not numbers alone that count. It's discipline and dedication too. One of the greatest battles of America, at least to us Texans, was the battle of the Alamo fought in 1836. There, 150 Texans, under the command of Col. William B. Travis, for thirteen days withstood the siege of 5,000 Mexican troops under General Antonio Lopez Santa Anna. They all died, but their resistance gave Sam Houston time to muster his army and win Texas her independence at San Jacinto a month later.

In the siege General Santa Anna and his forces had surrounded the little Spanish mission in San Antonio. One night a group of the Texans slipped out of the Alamo and stuffed the Mexican cannons full of mud. The next day when his army attempted to fire them, they exploded. When word came to General Santa Anna he exploded also. In a rage he said, "It is interesting, don't you think, that 150 men are so underwhelmed by our overwhelming forces that they send raiding parties against us. Do you think it's possible they know something about this army that I do not?"

Could it be that Satan and the forces of evil know something about us that we do not recognize ourselves? Could it be that he knows we lack the dedication and the discipline and the will to win?

We must realize that Jesus is not looking for spectators but for soldiers, not for admirers but for followers, not for applause but for obedience.

Iraeneus in the first century gave the march orders, "Christians, slaves, and soldiers, ask no questions." We are an army and we must be disciplined, dedicated, and obedient.

The church today fights for her life, but it is not the strength of our enemy that is holding us back. It is our own internal weakness. We are pressed with the menace of indifference and mediocrity.

When we become a Christian we don't just join a church, we join a cause — a cause that calls for and is worthy of their highest and their best.

A Lively, Reckless Confidence

The fourth essential for the church to be like an army is adequate resources. No army risks an offensive without enough to win. You dare not commit your forces to an invasion or an attack without resources adequate to see it through. You have to have enough to match the enemy — enough size, enough weight, enough power — to overcome the enemy or he will overcome and overpower you (Luke 14:31).

But, do we have enough resources? Some people are not sure. I say, "Yes." Jesus said, "The gates of hell will not stand against you." Obviously our resources are adequate.

The early church was not disheartened before all the impressive idolatry it encountered nor intimidated by the vastness of its undertaking. Its confidence lay in the gospel with which it was entrusted. Paul said it for them and for us, "I'm not ashamed of the gospel for it is the power of God."

Cornelius á Lapide tells us how Thomas Aquinas called upon Pope Innocent II once when the latter was counting a large sum of money. "You see, Thomas," said the Pope, "the church no longer has to say, 'Silver and gold have I none.'" "True, Holy Father," said Thomas, "but neither can she say, 'Arise and walk.'"

Our strength is never in our numbers or in our prosperity, but in the invincible powers of the gospel, the truth — God's kind of power.

Martin Luther, in his fight against the Roman church and the papacy, once said, "Hitherto I have been playing with the Pope; now I wage open war. I began this work in God's name; it will be ended without me, and by his might."

That's the spirit we need. Hitherto we have been playing at church. It's time for us to wage open war. And, as we do, we are assured that the victory is already won.

It almost goes without saying that if we are to march as a great army for the Lord, we must begin individually by enlisting in his service. I refer, of course, to the matter of becoming a Christian. First of all, each of us must make his own crucially important decision: Do I believe in Jesus Christ as the divine son of God? With that decision made, each of us is then ready to make known his faith by confessing Christ openly, by repenting of his past sins and turning the direction of his life toward the righteousness for which Christ lived and died, and then by being buried with him in baptism for the forgiveness of his past sins. Only then does Christ enroll us in his army.

Chapter 6

The Church, His Building

1 Peter 2:5

There is a famous story from ancient Sparta. A Spartan king boasted to a visiting monarch about the walls of Sparta. The visiting monarch looked around and he could see no walls. He said to the Spartan king, "Where are these walls about which you speak and boast so much?" The Spartan king pointed at his body guard of magnificent Spartan troops. "These," he said, "are the walls of Sparta, and every man of them a brick."

It is this idea that is behind the statement of Peter, "Ye also, as lively stones, are built up a spiritual house . . ." (1 Peter 2:5). Here, as in other places (Eph. 2:19-22, 1 Cor. 3:9-17), the church is viewed as a great building with Jesus Christ as the chief cornerstone and every Christian as a stone built into its walls.

The word "house" in the Greek refers to the inner sanctuary of the temple. It does not have reference to a structure in which a family lives, but to a temple where God dwells.

The church is not a building — though it meets in one and is compared to one. It is a "spiritual" house. It is not a house made of bricks and mortar, but of flesh and blood.

It is the living house of the living God. The church is people who rest on Christ, are indwelt by Christ, and who are cemented together by love for and commitment to Christ. Every time someone trusts Christ, another stone is quarried out of the pit of sin and cemented by God's grace into the walls of the church and thus they become a living part of the living house of the living God. Together we make a great spiritual edifice in whom our Lord dwells and through whom he is glorified.

What does this suggest to us about the nature of the church? What truths concerning the church does this convey?

- The church is founded on Christ.
- The church is united in Christ.
- The church is indwelt by Christ.

Stability and Flexibility

First, the church is founded on Christ. Jesus is called here "the chief cornerstone" of the church (1 Peter 2:4-6; Eph. 2:20; 1 Cor. 3:11).

It is doubtful that Peter could speak and think in terms of Jesus as the cornerstone without thinking of Jesus' words to him at Caesarea-Philippi. There Peter gave his great confession of faith, "Thou art the Christ, the son of the living God." Then Jesus said to him, "Thou art Peter (a small throwable stone), and upon this rock (a great ledge of stone) I will build my church; and the gates of hell shall not prevail against it" (Matt. 16:18).

Who or what is the rock to which Jesus refers? It is the confession Peter had just made about him. The church is not founded upon men, past or present. It is founded upon the divinity of Jesus Christ, on the truth of Peter's confession that Jesus is the Christ, the son of the living God.

Peter clarifies this by making the Lord, not himself, preeminent in this holy building which is the church. And Paul adds his testimony to this when he declares that the church is built upon the foundation of the apostles and prophets with Jesus himself as the chief cornerstone (Eph. 2:20). When Paul says the church is built on the foundation of the apostles and the prophets he has reference to their preaching, their proclamation of Christ. And again Paul declares, "For other foundation can no man lay than that (which) is laid, which is Jesus Christ" (1 Cor. 3:11).

The cornerstone was the main foundation stone of ancient buildings. It was the great stone put in the angle of the substructure where the walls meet. It was the stone upon which the stability of the whole building depended. If you took the cornerstone away the whole building would collapse in rubble; it was the cornerstone which held everything together.

If you go to the bedrock of our faith you will find Jesus Christ. As the cornerstone of a building holds it together, so it is Christ who holds the church together. We are not held together by our theology, or our politics, or our culture, but by him. He is the heart, the life, the soul of it. Without him the church could not stand. Without him the church would be just another gathering, just another assembly, just another audience. Without him it would crumble into ruins . . . and well it should.

The fact that it is founded on him gives to the church both stability and flexibility. It gives stability because Jesus is the same yesterday, today, and forever. We need that kind of stability today. We Americans are prone to believe that a thing is important only if it is recent; that the biggest news is the latest news. So I read two daily newspapers, I listen to the news flashes on the radio and television, and read several magazines every week just to keep up with the latest happenings.

Then on Sunday I go to church. There we sing the Doxology, "Praise God from whom all blessings flow." Some form of doxology has been sung by men and women at worship for at least twenty centuries. The hymns do not go back that far. But they go back far enough to be out of running for the hit song of the week. I sang them on Sunday morning when I was a boy. My mother sang them when she was just a girl, and her parents before her, and my pioneer great grandparents sang them when they crossed the Sabine River in covered wagons and settled land in Texas. My grandchildren and my great grandchildren and succeeding generations that I shall never know will sing them also. In the shifting sands of the changing times we need that kind of continuity and stability to our lives.

When the minister reads from the scriptures, especially from the Old Testament, he reads a book that goes back further than either the hymns or the doxology. It goes back thirty centuries — a thousand years before Christ. There is nothing new in what he reads to make the headlines. I heard the same passages in my youth. Men and women heard them generations into the past. My children and their children will hear them generations into the future. They are more than just a bridge between the past and the future, but they are that.

So in church I gain perspective. A thing need not be new to be of value or to be relevant. And we do a disservice to people by catering to those who think they do. Yesterday's newspaper did not have the first word and tomorrow's newspaper will not have the last word on many things important, and nothing eternal.

While the church has a certain unchanging quality about it, that does not mean that the church is stayed, archaic, or out of date. For, while founded on him, there is the possibility of great flexibility also. Leighton Ford tells of being in Los Angeles, California, several years ago when an earthquake hit the city. He was staying on the eleventh floor of a hotel when the first tremors came. He said, "The first thing I did was grab the bedpost and have my morning devotionals." Then he called the desk clerk and asked if he should leave the building or stay. The desk clerk replied, "Stay where you are. It the building goes, everything will go."

Later he asked a friend, "How do they build buildings to stand in California?" His friend replied, "First, they must go down to bedrock and lay the foundation. Then they must make the joints flexible so as to give with the stress."

Then Leighton said, "What a parable of the church. Built on the rock but flexible in methods and patterns."

Our message is always the same. We proclaim the

faith "once delivered unto the saints." But we remain constantly flexible to new methods and approaches in sharing the old story.

Woodpeckers or Termites

Second, the church is united in Christ. Upon the foundation of Jesus Christ believers are as "lively stones built up" into a spiritual house. The word "built" is a construction term. It refers to bringing various parts together and fitting them into a whole. That's what a mason or carpenter does. He takes various pieces of building material and fits them together to make a whole.

And that's what the church is — people from various professions, backgrounds, and walks in life who are united by love for and a commitment to Jesus Christ. This suggests that the church is a community, and the individual only finds his true place as he becomes a part of the group.

So long as a brick lies by itself it is useless for its intended purpose. It is only when it is built into a building that it does what it was made to do. It is the same with us. We are saved one by one, but one person does not make a church any more than one brick makes a building. We must then be joined together in right relationship to Christ, the foundation, and to one another.

Suppose in a time of war a man should say, "I wish to serve my country and to defend her from her enemies, but I don't want to join the military." If he tries to carry out that resolution alone, he can do very little. He can only do so by entering into the armed forces of his country. If a man is going to defend and support any great cause, he must associate himself with those who are like-minded with himself. It is so with the church.

We must, therefore, find our place in the church and fill it. Occasionally I find someone who says they are a Christian, they believe in Christ, but have no place in their lives for the church. They are like Winston Churchill, who was once asked by an admiring lady if he was a pillar of the church. Churchill replied that he was more like a fly-ing buttress: "I support it from the outside." The Bible knows nothing of that kind of churchless Christianity.

There are others who have only a casual relationship with the church. Bishop James Pike said some people have only a "sprinkling relationship" with the church: with water at baptism, rice at their wedding, and earth at death. To them it is a hatching, matching, and dispatching society.

There are still others who associate with the church only for what they can get out of it. That's all they think about. But we ought to go, not for what we can get out of it, but for what we can put into it. We go to church to add our prayers to the prayers of the saints through the ages. We go to church to add our praise to the mighty chorus of praise that goes up from others week by week. We go to church to add our testimony of the saving grace of God to the testimony of others. We go to church to add our wit-ness to the witness of the martyrs who have died for the faith. We go to church to add our influence to the influ-ence of millions who assemble every Lord's day. We may be just one brick, but that's what walls are made of . . . one brick on top of another.

And we do all we can to guard the unity of the church.

Church fights and division have been the curse of the church through the years. We must do everything in our power to avoid them. How can we proclaim to the world that we serve a God of love if we do not love and get along with one another?

Herb Bullock, a pastor friend of mine, told me that early in his ministry an elderly pastor said to him, "Son, don't ever pastor a church that has the name Harmony, Fellowship, or Friendship in it." Can you guess why? It is because behind those names there has invariably been division and strife.

All across America there are churches called "Harmony Baptist Church." If you'll drive further down the road you may see another sign that says, "New Harmony Baptist Church." And then still further another sign that says, "Greater Harmony Baptist Church." When that is so, you can rest assured there has not been much harmony in Harmony.

It is littleness among people that is so destructive and disruptive of the unity of the church. Mike Yaconelli, in the *Wittenberg Door* (December 1984/85), said, "The problem with the church today is not corruption. It is not institutionalism. No, the problem is far more serious than something like the minister running away with the organist. The problem is pettiness. Blatant pettiness."

The late Vance Havner said it like this, "The temple of truth has never suffered so much from woodpeckers on the outside as from termites on the inside." Don't ever be a part of that kind of dividing and damaging the living building of the living God.

I'm not saying that we must all agree on everything. As someone has said, "A church can't make harmony if all its members sing the same note." So we may sing different notes, but we attempt to sing them in harmony with one another.

Where God Dwells

Third, the church is indwelt by him. As we are built on Jesus Christ and are bound together in love, we become a spiritual temple in which God dwells. Paul expresses this when he writes, "And ye are . . . builded together for an habitation of God through the Spirit" (Eph. 2:20-22).

Sir Christopher Wren, the architect of St. Paul's Cathedral in London (the second largest church building in the world) walked among the workers one day and asked each one, "What are you doing?" One said, "Hewing stone." The second said, "I'm making three shillings a day." The third said, "Sir, I am building a cathedral."

That's what the church is about. We are not just teaching classes, ushering people to seats, or singing songs. We are by our worship, by our evangelism, by our service, and by our love building a great cathedral, a living monument to God's glory and grace.

The Holy Spirit does not haunt houses, he inhabits people (Acts 7:48-50). He dwells in the hearts of those who have trusted Christ (1 Cor. 6:19-20). In the Old Testament the temple was believed to be the dwelling place of God on earth. But today we know God dwells in his people.

Then he had a temple for his people. Now he has a people for his temple. In the Old Testament God was above us. In the New Testament God was beside us. In our day he is within us. God above us! God beside us! God within us!

Individually and collectively we are the temple of God on earth today. In that sense all churches should be "spirit-filled" fellowships. We have allowed the excesses of some churches to rob us of this claim. We have so associated the term with emotionalism, speaking in tongues, and fabricated miracles that we shy away from its use. But every church can legitimately claim to be "spirit-filled" and well they should.

The mark of a church being filled with the spirit is not tongues or miracles, but love and joy and holiness. As Dr. W. T. Conner, one of our great theologians, used to say, "What matters most is not how high you jump when you get the Holy Spirit, but how straight you walk when you come down."

The fact that we are the temple of God becomes a tremendous incentive for pure living. Because God's spirit dwells in us we have become a temple of God; and our very bodies are sacred (1 Cor 6:19-20).

Once when Augustine was tempted to plunge into the old life he said to himself, "Thou fool, does not thou know that thou are carrying God around in thee?" He was right. If you are a Christian, God is present within you. Talk about a mind-boggling concept!

We must take care not to quench the spirit within, but to be controlled and dominated by him. We must not have a house full of empty people. F. B. Myer was a famous preacher of the last generation. He said he had a dream on one occasion in which the Lord came to him and said, "F. B., give me all the keys to your life." So, he said, "I saw myself reaching down and handing him a ring of keys." Then God asked, "Are there any more?" And Myer replied, "No, Lord, except one to a small room in my life. But it's very small and not very important."

Then Myer said, in the dream the Lord handed him the keys back and said, "If I can't have all the keys I don't want any of them." Later Myer said, "In some Christians Christ is present. In others he is prominent. In a few he is preeminent." As he is preeminent in us we become the church, his house, in the fullest sense of the word.

There is in 1 Peter a contrast in what Christ means to believers and what he means to unbelievers. To the unbeliever he is the stone that was rejected (Matt. 21:42). He did not fit their plans, so they crucified him (1 Peter 2:4). But God raised him from the dead and made him to be the most important stone in the entire structure of his kingdom. So, to the unbeliever, to them, he was rejected. To us he is the elected (the chosen) and precious (honored). And those who believe in Christ, who esteem him as God does, will not be put to shame (1 Peter 2:6), but will share in the honor which God has bestowed on Christ (vs. 7a). Those who refuse to believe in Christ will find him to be a stone over which they stumble headlong into disaster (vs. 8).

The
Doctrines
of the
Church

Chapter 7

People of the Book

2 Peter 1:14-21

If I had to choose one phrase above all others to describe Baptists, it would be the phrase, "People of the Book." This is because historically, Baptists literally sprang from the Bible. In 1606, after a careful study of the New Testament and after years of spiritual conflict, John Smyth, a well-educated and deeply spiritual minister of the Church of England, concluded that the Church of England was not scriptural, so he separated from it. He soon assumed leadership of a separatist company in Gainsboro, England, along with Thomas Helwys and John Murton. But King James I was trying to keep his promise to drive all dissenters from the land and in 1609 the Gainsboro congregation was forced to flee to Amsterdam, Holland, where they established their first church.

Continued study of the New Testament convinced them that they were in error in rejecting only the government of the Church of England, and they must also reject their infant baptism. So, in 1609 Smith baptized himself and the rest of the company and organized what was to be the first Baptist church in history.

In 1834 in Hamburg, Germany, Johann Gerhard Oncken, who is known as the "Father of Continental Baptists," came to new life in Christ. Being without ecclesiastical guide, he and some of his friends shut themselves up to a study of the New Testament. A Baptist church resulted, and to this single congregation the Baptists of Germany largely trace their origin.

Baptists in Russia had a similar beginning. Lutheran missionaries went to Russia and preached; they left Bibles and then departed. With no guide but the Holy Spirit and the New Testament, a flourishing Baptist movement began in Russia that has continued unto today.

Our whole American Baptist missionary movement sprang directly from the New Testament. Adoniram Judson and Luther Rice were Congregational missionaries on their way to India. They knew once they arrived they would encounter a British Baptist missionary named William Carey and have to defend their practice of baptizing infants by sprinkling. Traveling on separate ships and each independent of the other, they began to read their New Testament to prepare their defense. In mid-ocean both became convinced that the Baptists were right and that the Bible taught the baptism of believers only, by immersion. When they landed in India, they promptly asked to be baptized, and they became Baptists.

Judson then remained in India as a missionary and Rice returned to the United States to organize missions support for these first Baptist missionaries from America.

Such has been the history of Baptists in many different countries. That is why we have always been known as a people of the book.

Because of our biblical roots it is important for us to understand the nature of scripture. Peter wrote of this when he, in the light of his approaching death, said the Christian message he proclaimed was not a collection of "cunningly devised fables," but the product of his own "eyewitness" experience (2 Peter 1:14-21).

The Greek word for "fables" means "myths" or "fairy tales." Peter affirmed that when he preached he was not relating concocted stories. He was relating things he had seen with his own two eyes and heard with his own two ears.

He then gave an example of one of these eyewitness experiences that impressed itself indelibly on him. It was the transfiguration of Jesus (Matt. 17:2).

In this experience Jesus took Peter, James, and John up into a mountain where he was transfigured before their very eyes. As he prayed his face shone with the brightness of heaven and they knew, by his very appearance, that he was the Messiah. Then, to confirm what they saw, there came a voice from heaven saying, "This is my beloved son in whom I am well pleased."

The word "eyewitness" means "an observer." What Peter related is what he actually saw and heard. It was not something he manufactured or concocted.

Then he made a most astonishing statement. He said, "We have also a more sure word of prophecy . . ." What could be surer than one's own experience? What could be more reliable than what you have seen with your own eyes and heard with your own ears? One thing — the word of God. Peter knew that our eyes can deceive us and our ears can mislead us. But God's word is absolutely trustworthy. It is more reliable than our experience. It is a sounder basis for faith than a single event out of our life.

Since God's word is true, Peter says we "would do well to take heed, as unto a light that shineth in a dark place . . ."

With his premise established he then declares, "No prophecy of scripture is of any private interpretation. For prophecy came not in old time by the will of man; but holy men of God spake as they were moved by the Holy Ghost."

The words "private interpretation" mean that the scriptures are not of human origin. They did not come about by personal discovery. Men did not set forth the ideas of scripture. They had their origin in God. He was the instigator; he was the motivator.

He further explains, scripture came as holy men of God were moved by the Holy Ghost. The Holy Spirit was the source of prophetic inspiration. Man did not originate the contents of scripture. It came to them by revelation. It was only mediated by human messengers.

In these verses we are allowed to see clearly the nature of scripture. Scripture is:

- the inspired word of God.
- the inerrant word of God.
- the illuminating word of God.

Holy Men and the Holy Ghost

First, the Bible is the inspired word of God. The apostle Paul wrote, "All scripture is given by inspiration of God, and is profitable for doctrine, for reproof, for correction, for instruction in righteousness;" (2 Tim. 3:16). The word "inspired" means "God-breathed."

But what does that mean? Peter helps us understand more clearly when he tells us that holy men of God spoke as they were "moved" by the Holy Ghost (vs. 21). The Greek word for "moved" means "to be picked up and borne along."

It is the same word used in Acts to describe what happened to the ship the apostle Paul was on while traveling to Rome. It was caught in a ferocious storm, and it looked as though it would be dashed against the rocks. In an effort to save the ship and their own lives, the sailors threw the cargo overboard to lighten the load, wrapped ropes under the hull to strengthen it, lowered the sails and just drifted before the wind (Acts 27:17). The word "driven" and the word "moved" are translations of the same Greek word.

In the same way that the wind pushed that ship and drove it forward, so the breath of God came upon holy men and impelled them, picked them up and bore them along in this work. He moved them to write the words of holy scripture.

The Bible writers were not self-starters. They were not original thinkers. They were men upon whom the spirit of God came with such force that they were compelled to write what they wrote. Like Jeremiah, God's word was as fire in their bones, and they could not keep it to themselves.

Inspiration, then, means the Holy Spirit of God was the source and the force of prophetic writing. It means that God guided and guarded the writers of scripture so that they gave to us the message he wanted us to hear. Peter thus emphasizes the dual authorship of scripture, the partnership between God and men. The formula for inspiration is: Holy Spirit times holy men equals the Holy Bible.

What is the extent of inspiration? Peter uses two negatives to help us understand. He writes, "No prophecy of scripture is of any private interpretation" (v. 20). And, "Prophecy came not by the will of man" (v. 21). Those two negatives, "no" and "not" are absolute negatives in the Greek. What Peter is saying is, "No part of scripture is of human origin." And, "Nothing whatsoever of prophecy came by the will of men."

Logically, now, if no part of it came from man, then all of it came from God. This is the affirmation of Paul when he writes that "all scripture is given by inspiration of God" (2 Tim. 3:16). The construction of that sentence in the Greek is such that the word "all" means "every single part of the whole." What then is the extent of inspiration? It is as broad as scripture itself. Every single part of it is inspired.

Some people want to believe that parts of the Bible are inspired and other parts are not. They want to pick and choose the parts they believe are true. But, if I believe a part of the Bible and I reject a part of the Bible, it is not the Bible I believe, but myself.

How did God inspire these men? What method did he use? We are not told. We are left to struggle with that for ourselves. There are two theories: the dictation theory and the dynamic theory. The dictation theory is plenary verbal (every word) inspiration. It says God dictated scripture and men wrote word for word what he told them.

The dynamic theory is the inspiration of ideas. It suggests that God impressed truths on men and allowed them to choose their own words in expressing it.

Let me illustrate. At the Annuity Board where I work I have access to a number of secretaries. If I dictate a letter it does not matter which secretary I use. The letter will come out the same because I tell her word for word what to write.

However, if I ask any one of them to write a letter for me, and tell them in general terms what I want it to say, the letters would all come out different because they would use their own style and words. The letter would say what I wanted said but in their words.

The latter method is dynamic and is the method I believe God used in giving us holy scripture. This is the only way to account for the different styles and unique phrases of the various biblical writers.

For example, Jesus said, "It is harder for a rich man to enter into heaven than for a camel to go through the eye of a needle." When Matthew recorded that, the word he used for needle was the Greek word for an ordinary sewing needle. But when Luke, who was a physician by profession, recorded the saying, the Greek word he used for needle was the word for a surgical needle. The same truth is expressed by both men, but they use different words — their own words.

The thing to focus on, however, is not the method but the product. I believe whatever method he used, God so guided the human authors that the results in the whole and in the parts are exactly what God desired to be expressed. That is inspiration.

Without Mixture of Error

Second, the Bible is the inerrant word of God. If the Bible is inspired, it must be inerrant. It cannot be, at least for me, the word of God and be full of mistakes. The God of this universe is the God of truth, and he cannot breathe error.

Some people insist on using the word "inerrant" to describe the Bible. But the phrase I and most Baptists have preferred to use throughout the years is "truth without mixture of error." At the 1963 meeting of the Southern Baptist Convention we adopted our present "Baptist Faith and Message." The first article of that confession says of the Bible, "It has God for its author, salvation for its end, and truth without mixture of error for its matter." But that statement was not coined by the 1963 convention. It was borrowed from the 1925 "Confession of Faith" which was, in turn, taken from a confession written in 1833.

But according to the late Dr. Hugh Wamble, professor of church history at Midwestern Seminary, the statement is much older than that. He researched it and found it first in a bound volume of letters written by the English philosopher John Locke (1632-1704).

An Anglican minister (Richard King) had asked how a "young gentleman" may "attain a true knowledge of the Christian religion, in the full and just extent of it." On August 25, 1703, Locke gave "a short and plain answer," saying: "Let him study the body of the scripture, especially the New Testament. Therein are contained the words of eternal life. It has God for its author; salvation for its end; and truth, without any mixture of error, for its matter."

One may see Locke's letter in *The Works of John Locke, in Ten Volumes* (11th edition, London: W. Otridge and Son, 1812), X, 306, or other editions of the "Works."

So, the phrase, "truth without mixture of error," came not from a preacher or theologian, but from a philosopher. And it has served Baptists well for over 150 years.

Why do we prefer, "truth without mixture of error," to "inerrant" with reference to the Bible? For two reasons. First, because the Bible must be interpreted. We must interpret the Bible because of the gaps between biblical times and ours. There are at least three of them:

- There is the language gap. The scriptures were given to us in Hebrew, Aramaic, and Greek. Since no two languages have exactly the same words to express ideas, it is impossible to translate the scriptures literally. Differences in the meanings of words and expressions often lead to confusion.

- There is the cultural gap. The Bible came from an eastern, pre-scientific, agrarian culture. Our culture is largely western, scientific, and urban. They had ways of understanding and explaining their world, which are sometimes much different from ours.

- There is the time gap. We are separated from biblical events by thousands of years.

For each of these gaps, the answer is interpretation.
Interpretation is the bridge we need for the biblical message to cross over to us today and we can make mistakes
in our interpretation. The scriptures are inerrant, but our
interpretations are not.

The second reason we prefer to say "truth without
mixture of error" is we do not presently possess an inerrant
Bible nor have we ever seen one. When inerrancy is
claimed for the scriptures, it does not refer to the King
James Version or to any other translation of the Bible —
ancient or modern. It refers to the original manuscripts,
the autographs, none of which exists today. So, belief in
inerrancy is a faith assumption.

The copies of scripture we have today all contain some
minor errors. For example, 2 Samuel 10:18 and 1 Chroni-
cles 19:18 are parallel accounts of the same historical
event, David's defeat of the Syrian army and the death of
Shobach, the captain of the Syrian army. One account
records that David slew 700 chariot drivers and the other
account records that he slew 7,000. Which one is correct?
We do not know. But they can't both be correct.

Again, when Jesus came down from the Mount of
Transfiguration, he found his disciples baffled by a young
man possessed of demons. They had tried to heal the
young man without success. Jesus then healed the boy and
said to his disciples, according to the King James Version
of the Bible, "This kind comes out only by prayer and fasting" (Matt. 17:21). However, in the oldest manuscripts

this verse is not found. Apparently some copyists added it in by accident or in an effort to interpret what the copyist thought Jesus meant.

And again, in the Bible you possess, the last chapter of the book of Mark may contain twenty verses. But, scholars generally agree that the book of Mark ends with verse eight because the last twelve verses are not found in other manuscripts. However, ending the book of Mark at verse eight would be so abrupt that it is generally believed the original ending was lost and the present ending was added by a later editor.

All good study Bibles, including the Criswell Study Bible, the Ryrie Study Bible, and the Open Bible point out these mistakes in their footnotes.

How did mistakes come about? How do we account for these errors in our translation of the Bible? They are the mistakes of copyists. How did they happen? In the days before printing presses, the scriptures were copied by hand by scribes. Sometimes scribes made notes in the margins of their manuscripts as they studied, just as we do. Then, when the scriptures were recopied at a later date, those notes were sometimes mistaken for a part of the original text. After the invention of the printing press, notes written in the margins were no longer mistaken for scripture and those kinds of errors no longer happen.

They occurred in other ways also. Some were of the eye and some were of the ear. As monks copied the scriptures from old scrolls, they would occasionally look back to the page they were copying and miss a line or a word. Or sometimes one monk would read aloud a manuscript

while another copied it and the copyist would not hear correctly what was read.

"Can I, then," you ask, "trust the Bible?" Absolutely!
All the mistakes in the Bible are minor and do not affect
any significant teaching of scripture. Today, we have literally thousands of manuscripts of the Old and New Testa-
ments. Some of the New Testament manuscripts date back
to the fourth century, and we have one fragment of John
that is once removed from the original. Through studies of
these old Greek and Hebrew texts, scholars have virtually
restored the New Testament text for us.

In fact, of the 5,000 Greek manuscripts which have
been found, it has been determined by cybernetics and the
use of computers that in comparison with our present New
Testament books, less than one percent of all texts is at
variance — less than one percent can be questioned.

Peter gives emphasis to the accuracy of scripture when
he relates his experience of seeing Jesus transfigured and
hearing the voice of God on the Mount of Transfiguration.
Then he adds that God has given us a "more sure" word of
prophecy than that.

By making use of the comparative, Peter is claiming a
degree of certainty for the scriptures unmatched by anything in man's experience. Peter knew our eyes can deceive us and our ears can mislead us. But God's word is
absolutely trustworthy. It is totally reliable. It is the one
firm, stable foundation for our faith.

There is a message here for us. Don't build your faith
on experience — not what you believe about angels, about
miracles, about giving, about life after death, or even

morality. Build it on the sure word of God. The basis of most heresy is people building their faith on their experiences and making them normative for the Christian life. Experiences can be wrong. If your experience does not square with scripture, it is your experience, not the scripture, that is wrong.

A Lamp and a Light

Third, the Bible is the illuminating word of God. Since this book is inspired and inerrant, it is also illuminating. Peter says we should "take heed" to it as unto a light that shines in a "dark place." The Greek word translated "dark" means "murky." That is an apt description of our age.

We live in a time of moral confusion. Young people are sleeping around, athletes are abusing drugs, men and women are living together out of wedlock. Drunkenness, pornography, and homosexuality are accepted practices. Celebrities are becoming criminals and public officials are on the take. It is a dark day in which we live.

In the midst of our moral murkiness, God has not left us to grope in the dark. He gave us the Bible to teach us what to believe and how to live. It was given as a light to guide us. The psalmist said it best, "Thy word is a lamp unto my feet and a light unto my path" (Ps. 119:105).

During the televangelist scandal of a few years ago, a comedian on the Johnny Carson show quipped one night, "I understand television evangelists are trying to develop a code of ethics for their profession." Then he lifted a Bible high above his head and waved it saying, "I thought they already had one." They do. And so do we. And the time has come for us to stop groping in the dark and start walking in the light.

During the French Revolution prisoners packed the dark dungeon of the Bastille. Each day only a small sliver of light peeked in for a brief time.

One prisoner had a Bible, but the short light was too high for him to read by. A decision was made. "We will lift you up on our shoulders with the book so that you can read . . . our only request to you is that when you return to our dark world, give us the message you got while you were in the light."

Helping those in spiritual darkness to discover the light which reveals God and rescues from death is the responsibility of every believer.

This then, is the nature of scripture: It is the inspired, infallible, illuminating word of God. I don't understand it all, but I stand on it all.

But, you say, that's old fashioned. Yes, and so is the sun. But without it, men grope in darkness. So is the air, but without it men gasp and die. So is water, but without it men go mad.

In the midst of the complexities of life, don't forget the Holy Bible. Believe it, read it, and heed it. It holds the key to life.

Chapter 8

The Priesthood of
Every Believer

1 Peter 2:5, 9

When I first met Dr. Mary Gray she was campus
physician and psychiatrist at Stephen F. Austin University,
Nacogdoches, Texas. After retirement she decided to give
her remaining years to medical missions. Under the aus-
pices of the Foreign Mission Board of the Southern Baptist
Convention she went to Zimbabwe to work in our Baptist
hospital. From there she wrote me, "The people of Africa
where I serve all believe God created the heavens and the
earth. But, they do not believe they can approach him."

Belief in the unapproachableness of God is deeply
imbedded in man. It is from this feeling that the idea of
priesthood first emerged. Men universally have felt they
have offended the power to whom they are responsible
and to whom they must give an account. But they did
not and do not feel they can approach him. To them it is
the priest or the witch doctor of the medicine man who

connects them with the unapproachable God.

Long before the Lord established the Jewish priesthood, a priesthood existed in other religions. Abraham, who lived 800 years before Moses, gave tithes to Melchizedek, "a priest of the most high God." When Moses fled Egypt he went to the land of Midian where he married Zipporah, the daughter of Jethro, a priest of the Midianites. It would be years later before God gave the law to Moses and officially established a priesthood in Israel. The tribe of Levi would be the priestly tribe and the high priests would come from the family of Aaron.

The function of the priest was to maintain worship in the tabernacle in the wilderness, and later in the temple, and to teach the people God's law. They were men who had a special access to God and through whom the people approached God. By Jesus' day this concept of a priesthood was firmly implanted in the minds of the people.

The temple was the central place of worship in Jewish life. And the heart of temple worship was the inner sanctuary, where they believed God dwelt. It was a large room divided by a huge veil, sixty feet long, thirty feet wide, and three inches thick. One part of the room was the holy place. The other, the holy of holies. Into the holy place the priest went daily to offer sacrifices for the people. Into the holy of holies, which represented the immediate presence of God, the high priest went once a year to offer a blood atonement for the sins of the whole nation.

The inner sanctuary was surrounded by a series of courtyards in which the people gathered to worship. When a Jewish worshipper entered the temple he would pass to the court of the Gentiles, or to the court of the women, or to the court of the Israelites, but there he must stop. Into the court of the priest he could not go; no nearer to the presence of God could he come. Only the priests could go there. And behind the veil, into the holy of holies, only the high priest could go.

Among the miraculous things that happened when Jesus died on the cross was that the veil in the temple, that huge curtain that separated the holy place from the holy of holies, was rent from top to bottom, signifying that the way into the presence of God was now open to all people (Matt. 27:51). The veil was not torn from bottom to top as though torn by man. It was torn from top to bottom as though God reached down and tore it, signaling that all believers now have equal "access in one spirit to the father" (Eph. 2:18).

The rending of the veil in the temple signified the beginning of a theological revolution.

- It meant through Jesus Christ, the new and living way to God was now open to every believer, however simple and unlettered he may be.

- It meant the Jewish priests were out of work. They were in the ranks of the unemployed.

- It means Christianity is essentially a lay movement. Power and prestige are not concentrated in a few. Pastors are to give leadership but they are not priests in the official sense of the word. The word "priest" is never once applied to a minister, pastor, elder, or a bishop in the New Testament.

Though priestly functions may be exercised, they have no power as intercessors that does not belong to every believer. In no sense has the church, or any church, an official priesthood in the New Testament.

- It means there are no second class citizens in the kingdom of God. We are all equal in his sight.

Milton Cunningham, chaplain of Baylor University, tells when he served as a missionary in Africa, he was seated at a banquet table with the Litunga Barotseland and members of the family. He was one of the paramount royal chiefs of Africa. His kingdom was in the western province of Zambia. Milton said, "I was seated next to a young African lady about 20 years old who was a member of the Litunga family."

"I said to her, 'Tell me, where are you in the possibility of ascendancy to the throne to be the queen?' I'll never forget her answer. She turned to me and said, 'Oh, I'm just an ordinary princess.'"

Have you ever met an ordinary princess? There are no ordinary princesses. All princesses are special. Just so, there are no ordinary Christians. We are all royalty. The scriptures declare, "He hath made us kings and priests" unto God (Rev. 5:10).

The New Testament clearly teaches that every born again believer is appointed a priest. And, we have direct access to God through the mediation of Christ without the necessity of an earthly priest.

That's the emphasis of Peter when he declares that we are "an holy priesthood, to offer up spiritual sacrifices acceptable to God by Jesus Christ". . . and that we are "a royal priesthood, an holy nation, a peculiar people; that we should show forth the praises of him who hath called (us) out of darkness and into his marvelous light" (1 Peter 2:5, 9).

What does the priesthood of every believer mean in practical terms? It means three things:

- We are free to approach God directly.

- We are obligated to offer spiritual sacrifice to God individually.

- We are responsible to build bridges between God and men personally.

Direct Distance Dialing

First, the priesthood of every believer means we don't have to go through anyone's switchboard to connect with God. Through what Jesus did on the cross, direct distance dialing to heaven is now possible for everyone.

From Calvary Baptist Church in Washington, D.C., comes a wonderful story. When Chief Justice Charles Evans Hughes walked the aisle of the church to present himself for membership, a Chinese laundry man from the neighborhood Chinatown, came seeking membership at the same time. It has been said that the pastor commented, "The ground is wondrously level at the foot of the cross." It is, and we all come to God just alike.

Walter Shurden tells about a Baptist pastor invited by a pulpit committee to meet with the deacons of the church for a preliminary interview. After the usual light chitchat, they got down to business.

One of the deacons, a delightful wholesale grocer, looked at the candidate and said, "Sir, what one question do you want most to get answered from us?" Almost immediately the prospective pastor shot back, "I want to know if you have a free and open pulpit. Do I have the freedom to say from this pulpit what I honestly think God wants me to say?"

The deacon who asked the question responded, "Yes," he said, slowly and deliberately. "We have a free pulpit." Then he added, "But, we also have a free pew." Hurrah for him!

We Baptists are free people. Free to approach God without human intermediary. Free to believe or free to reject the gospel. Free to pray directly to God. Free to confess our own sins. Free to govern our own churches. Free to interpret scripture for ourselves.

This does not mean you can believe anything and still be a Baptist. The doctrine of the priesthood of the believer in no way gives license to misinterpret, explain away, demythologize, or extrapolate out elements of the supernatural from the Bible. We have no right to twist, to ignore, to pick and choose parts of the Bible. But by using good principles of interpretation and relying on the Holy Spirit, we have the right to interpret scripture for ourselves.

Jude, in his epistle, encouraged us to earnestly contend for the faith that was "once" delivered to the saints. The Greek word translated "once" literally means "once and for all." The body of Christian faith was given to us full and complete. It needs no additions and allows no subtractions.

The sum of human knowledge has increased remarkably since the first century. It took from the beginning of time till the birth of Christ to accumulate a sum of human knowledge. It then took from the time of Jesus to 1760 for that sum to double. By 1880, just 120 years later, it doubled again. By 1914, 34 years later, it doubled again. By 1941, 27 years later, it doubled again. By 1952, just 11 years later, it doubled again. By 1959, just 7 years later, it doubled again. By 1962, just 3 years later, it doubled again. Since 1985 the sum of human knowledge has been doubling every six months, and now in even less time.

But with all this new information available, the gospel has not changed one bit. God's revelation through Jesus Christ is full and complete. It needs to be restudied, re-expressed, and reapplied in every generation. But there is nothing to be added to it nor taken from it.

"But should I," you ask, "believe the same things my grandfather believed?" Yes, emphatically so! If he rightly understood the scriptures, you can safely believe the same thing your grandfather believed about God, Christ, salvation, and eternity. There is an unchanging quality about our faith. It is related to us in scripture. And we are free to read, understand, and apply that for ourselves.

All on the Altar

Second, we are obligated to offer spiritual sacrifices to God for ourselves. According to Peter we are a holy priesthood "to offer up spiritual sacrifices" that are acceptable to God by Christ Jesus. From his childhood Peter had been taught the importance of making sacrifices to God. He had been instructed that, at the appointed time and in the accepted manner, he was to take an animal to the priest. The priest in turn would offer that animal as a sacrifice on the altar of the temple as a symbol of his dedication to God. When Peter became a Christian he ceased to make animal sacrifices. The reason was he realized Christ was the lamb of God to take away the sins of the world. He knew that the sinless son of God had been offered "once and for all" as a sacrifice, not upon the altar of the temple, but upon the cross of Calvary. And so effective had been the sacrifice of Jesus that never again would mankind have to offer up the blood of bulls and goats to atone for their sins (Heb. 9:23-28).

But while Peter ceased to make animal sacrifices unto God, he never suggested that God had abolished the principle of sacrifice in true worship. No! God has not abolished the principle of sacrifice; he has simply changed the form. God is no longer interested in physical sacrifices. What he wants is a spiritual one.

What are the spiritual sacrifices we are to offer unto God? The Bible lists four: the sacrifice of penitence; the sacrifice of praise, the sacrifice of our possessions; and the sacrifice of our person.

- There is the sacrifice of penitence. David wrote, "Thou desirest not sacrifice; else would I give it: thou delightest not in burnt offering. The sacrifices of God are a broken spirit: a broken and contrite heart, O God, thou wilt not despise" (Ps. 51:16-17). What God wants from us is not some *thing*, but a heart repentant over our sin.

- Another sacrifice we bring to God is the sacrifice of praise. "By him therefore let us offer the sacrifice of praise to God continually, that is, the fruit of our lips giving thanks to his name" (Heb. 13:15).

This, I believe, refers to both prayer and music. What power music has to move the hearts of men! And what power it has, I believe, to touch the heart of God!

God sent singers upon the earth
With songs of sadness and of mirth
That they might touch the hearts of men,
And bring them back to heaven again.

Music is not to be a meaningless ritual. It is not to be entertainment. It is a sacrifice — a presentation of the fruit of our lips to God. That's why the emphasis in church needs to be placed more on participation than on performance. It is not enough to have a beautiful choir render beautiful music. We do not come to watch or listen to them perform. We come to participate. We come to offer the sacrifice of praise to the Lord ourselves.

- And there is the sacrifice of our possessions. The writer of Hebrews again encourages us to "do good and to communicate" for with such sacrifices God is well pleased (Heb. 13:16).

The Greek word translated "communicate" means to share. Through the giving of our gifts we offer to God a sacrifice.

The church at Philippi made financial contributions to the apostle Paul's ministry. He describes their gift as "an odor of sweet smell, a sacrifice acceptable, well pleasing to God" (Phil. 4:18). With those words Paul invested their gift with all the sacredness of an Old Testament sacrifice.

Giving to the church is not just a means of paying the bills. It is a means of offering sacrifices unto the Lord. That is why we entitle it "the offering."

- The final sacrifice we bring to God is the sacrifice of our person. The apostle Paul appealed to us to "present" our bodies as a living sacrifice to the Lord (Rom. 12:1). The word "present" means "to put at one's disposal." It is a technical term which was used to describe the work of the Levitical priest as he offered a sacrifice unto God.

The word "bodies" means our "whole selves." It includes our ears, eyes, hands, lips, feet — our entire being. The words "living sacrifice" refer to a sacrifice that is alive as opposed to one that is dead. God doesn't want a dead animal; God wants a living person. He wants you and me.

At Baylor Medical Center in Dallas, Texas, there is a famous display of hands. The collection is located on the main floor of the Jonsson Hospital at the Center — bronze cast hands of various famous people, each made by Dr. Adrian E. Flatt, an orthopedic surgeon who bases his nationwide practice in Dallas.

Some of the famous hands sculpted there are Charles Schultz of "Peanuts" fame, artist Norman Rockwell, Walt Disney, Mickey Mantle and Joe DiMaggio, Arnold Palmer and Wilt Chamberlain. The largest hands belong to the late Andre Roussimoff, known more popularly as the wrestler Andre the Giant. And, of course, the display being in Dallas, you can see the hands of Roger Staubach and Tom Landry.

Among all these famous hands of imminent people, you might ask, "Where are the hands of Jesus?" In this Baptist hospital, where are his hands? The answer is, "At the end of your arms." When you look at your own hands you see his.

"He has no hands but our hands," the poet says, "to do his work today." And, he wants those hands, as well as every other part of our being, laid on the altar in dedication to him.

Reach Up in Faith — Reach Out in Love

Third, we have the responsibility to bring other people to God. The Latin word for priest is "pontifex," which means a bridge builder. As believer priests we are to build bridges between God and men.

Martin Luther was right when he said, "It is our responsibility to 'reach up in faith to God' but also to 'reach out in love to others.'" We are priests before God and priests to our neighbors.

We must realize we will never win our world to Christ at 11:00 on Sunday morning. We can't be content to sit around and sing, "Just As I Am" to one another. John Wesley said, "A man must have friends or make friends; for no one ever went to heaven alone."

We must busy ourselves building bridges for sharing our faith where we live, where we work, and where we spend our leisure time. Every Christian this side of heaven ought to be concerned about every lost person this side of hell.

As our own priests we must come to God for ourselves. There is no such thing as proxy religion. Stand-ins won't work. Spectator religion is out. The choice is ours. God has no grandchildren. The responsibility goes with the privilege. I urge you to take responsibility for your life. No one else can choose for you. No one else can stop you from choosing. You are free and you are responsible.

I have in my office a replica of the sign Harry Truman kept on his desk during the years of his presidency. It was given to me by one of my trustees on a visit to Independence, Missouri, years ago. The sign reads, "The buck stops here." It constantly and consistently reminded Harry Truman that he was ultimately responsible for all decisions involving national government. The Bible teaches that, in similar manner, the final responsibility for our relationship with God rests on our own shoulders. There is no one else who can make that decision for you.

The final and supreme act of a priest is for us to offer our lives to the Lord. As the apostle Paul spoke of his life and death he described it in terms of a sacrifice. He said, "I am now ready to be offered," i.e., I am now ready to make my final oblation to God. I am ready to carry out my final act as a priest. So he offered up his life as a sacrifice to God. And we can all do that.

The poet Christina Rossetti put it well:

What can I give him poor as I am?
If I were a shepherd I'd give him a lamb.
If I were a wise man I'd do my part,
Yet what can I give him? Give him my heart.

Exercise your privilege and responsibility as a believer priest. Give your life to Christ now.

Chapter 9

Soul Competency

Hebrews 8:10-11

Recently I served on my first jury. The case was a competency trial. Our charge was to determine if, in our opinion, the defendant had the mental capacity to know right from wrong, and thus to be held responsible for his actions. We were not to rule on his guilt or innocence of a crime. In fact, we didn't even know of what crime he was accused. We were just to decide if he was competent, if he had the capacity to be responsible for what he did.

Two witnesses were called, one for the defense and one for the prosecution. The first was a psychologist for the defendant. The second was a psychiatrist for the prosecution. The psychiatrist convinced us that the defendant knew the judicial system well. He had been in and out of jail often. And he preferred a mental institution to prison, so he was faking incompetence.

It took us five minutes to declare him competent and, thus, responsible for his actions. That meant he must stand trial for the crime of which he was accused.

This experience brought new meaning to me of one of our most basic Baptist beliefs — soul competency. Soul competency is the belief that God created us with a capacity to know him personally and to respond to him directly. It is the belief that religious faith is a personal matter between the worshipper and God and that we are capable of dealing with God for ourselves, without interference from or the aid of any human intermediary.

So basic, so fundamental is this doctrine that E. Y. Mullins, one of our most respected scholars of the past, called soul competency an "axiom of religion," i.e., a self evident, a universally recognized truth.

While it should be self-evident, to many this obviously is not. There are those who say, "We cannot pray directly to God. We should pray to and through the saints." They say, "We cannot confess our sin directly to God. We should confess our sins to a priest and he will grant us forgiveness in God's behalf." And they say, "We cannot interpret scripture for ourselves. The church must do that for us." "The church," they say, "is to the scriptures what the Supreme Court is to the Constitution. It is the duly authorized interpreter of scripture."

Members of one religious sect said of their church, "When our leaders speak, the thinking has been done. When they propose a plan, it is God's plan. When they point the way, there is no other which is safe." (*The Mormon Corporate Empire*, John Heinerman and Anson Shupe.)

And in another statement they warned: "God will do nothing regarding his work except through his own duly appointed prophets . . . they will give us the Lord's word in no uncertain terms as God makes it known . . . let us follow them and avoid being led astray." (*Church News*, 1991.)

No true Baptist would ever accept such beliefs. We would never allow another person to do our thinking for us, to determine God's will for us, or to restrict God's working through a select few. We cling tenaciously to the right of private judgment and freedom from ecclesiastical superiors for ourselves and all believers. We all have the same spiritual privilege and responsibility. To attempt to deprive anyone of this right is tyranny.

Our belief in soul competency is based on three things: the creation of God, the incarnation of Christ, and the invitation of the Spirit. We believe that God is a person of intelligence, power, and love. And we believe that man is the special creation of God, made in his image.

What does it mean to say man is made in the image of God? It means man has intelligence, conscience and a soul. We are rational, moral, and spiritual.

Man has intelligence. Animals act primarily by instinct. But man can think and reason objectively. Try teaching geometry to an elephant or astronomy to an eagle or theology to a dog. They can never learn it. But the most primitive savage from the darkest jungle can learn all three. That's because he is like God. He has intelligence.

More than that, man has a conscience. He has the voice of God within. He has an inborn sense of right and wrong. A dog can bite you or a bull can gore you, and feel no remorse. But man is different.

And man is spiritual. God has "planted eternity" in our hearts (Ecc. 3:11). There is in us a sense of something above and beyond us, an awareness of God.

Soul competency is also based on the revelation of God. God has come to us in Christ. This implies a kinship between God and man. The incarnation is the great historical expression of competency. It implies that God can communicate and man can receive revelation. Why else would God reveal himself to us if we did not have the capacity to respond?

And, the invitation of the Holy Spirit implies competency. Throughout scripture the Lord repeatedly invites us to come to him. Listen to his last great invitation: "The spirit and the bride say come. And let him that is athirst come. And whosoever will, let him take the water of life freely" (Rev. 22:17). Why would God invite us to come personally, individually, if we were not capable of knowing him personally and responding to him directly?

There is no other doctrine for which Baptists have stood so firmly and consistently as this. And there is no other belief quite so central and quite so important to us as this. It is Baptists' greatest contribution to history.

The writer of Hebrews speaks of our competency when he contrasted the old covenant and the new covenant (Heb. 8:10-11). In the old covenant God spoke to men through the prophets and men approached God through the priests. But in the new covenant each person has direct access to God. He quotes Jeremiah: "But this shall be the covenant that I will make with the house of Israel; after those days, said the Lord, I will put my law in their inward parts, and write it in their hearts; and will be their God, and they shall be my people. And they shall teach no more every man his brother, saying, Know the Lord: for they shall all know me, from the least of them unto the greatest of them, saith the Lord: for I will forgive their iniquity, and I will remember their sin no more" (Jer. 31:33-34).

The scriptures remind us that all persons, from the least to the greatest, are now on equal footing before the Lord. No one is exclusive and no one is excluded. Individualism is the distinct mark of the new covenant as contrasted with the old. From this basic truth flow three other great truths. They are:

- We are competent to deal directly with God in all matters of religion.
- We are competent to decide for ourselves in matters of conscience.
- We are competent to discern God's will for ourselves in matters of the church.

The Right to Access

First, we are competent to deal directly with God in matters of religion. There is no special class with God. There is no person or group, whether priest or bishop, pope or preacher, who has more access to him than another and through whom we must approach God. And, no one has the right or the ability to act religiously for another. Only Jesus stands between us and God. As the apostle Paul wrote, "For there is one God, and one mediator between God and men, the man Jesus Christ" (1 Tim. 2:5).

Jesus, by virtue of his death, burial, and resurrection, is our high priest. Listen to the writer of Hebrews: "Seeing then that we have a great high priest, that is passed into the heavens, Jesus the Son of God . . . let us therefore come boldly unto the throne of grace, that we may obtain mercy, and find grace to help in time of need" (Heb. 4:14-16). Through Christ the way to God is now open to us.

Beyond that, all of us as believers are now priests. In the words of Peter, "Ye . . . are an holy priesthood, to offer up spiritual sacrifices, acceptable to God by Jesus Christ". . . and "Ye are . . . a royal priesthood, . . . that ye should show forth the praises of him who hath called you out of the darkness into his marvelous light" (1 Peter 2:5, 9). This priesthood of the believer is the religious expression of soul competency.

What this means practically is that we are competent to pray directly to God. The apostles asked Jesus to teach them to pray. In response to their request he taught them, "After this manner pray ye, Our Father, which art in heaven . . ." (Luke 11:1-2). That's about as direct as you can get.

As our own priest we are competent to confess our sins directly to God (Matt. 6:12). A Baptist and Roman Catholic were talking in order to try to understand one another's faith better. The Roman Catholic asked the Baptist, "What do you do when you sin?" The Baptist replied, "I confess my sins to God."

The Baptist then asked the Roman Catholic, "And what do you do when you sin?" The Catholic replied, "I confess my sins to the priest." The Baptist asked, "Who does the priest confess his sins to?" And the Catholic replied, "He confesses his sins to the bishop."

The Baptist then asked, "Who does the bishop confess

his sins to?" The Catholic replied, "He confesses his sins to the cardinal."

The Baptist then asked, "Who does the cardinal confess his sins to?" The Catholic replied, "He confesses his sins to the pope."

The Baptist then asked, "Well, who does the pope confess his sins to?" The Catholic said, "He confesses his sins to God."

The Baptist then said, "Huh! I guess that means the pope is a Baptist."

As our own priest we are competent to interpret scripture for ourselves. The apostle Paul commended the Christians of Berea because they heard his preaching readily and then "searched the scriptures" to see if what he said was true (Acts 17:11).

The Berean brethren didn't accept what Paul said as gospel without question, and Paul acknowledged that they were competent to read and understand scripture on their own. Just so, we Baptists believe God has given to each of us the capacity to understand and interpret the Bible for ourselves.

As believers we may differ in our understanding of, and beliefs about, many things in scripture. We don't all agree on how creation came about. Some believe the world was created in six literal days and some believe it was created in six geological periods of time. The Hebrew word for day, yom, lends itself to either interpretation.

We don't all agree on inspiration. Some people believe in plenary, verbal, inspiration, i.e., every word in the Bible was given to us directly by God. Others believe that inspiration was more dynamic, i.e., that God inspired ideas and allowed men to express that truth in their own words.

We don't all believe the same things about the second coming. Some believe that Jesus will come in the air and his church will be raptured from the earth. This will be followed by seven years of tribulation, in which the unbelieving Jews will be saved. Afterwards Jesus will return, set up an earthly kingdom, and rule on the earth for 1,000 years. Then the judgment will take place and the eternal order will begin.

Others believe that Jesus' coming will be a single event. When it occurs the resurrection will take place and the judgment will be held and the eternal order will begin all at once.

I preached a sermon on the second coming in a former pastorate and the next week one of my Sunday School teachers called and said, "Pastor, I don't believe the way you believe about the second coming. Should I resign my class?" I said, "By no means! Teach your class what you believe. But tell them that there are other people who believe the Bible as much as you do, who interpret things differently."

We both believed in the personal, visible, victorious return of Christ. We both believed in a final judgment. We both believed in heaven and hell. But our understanding of all the events surrounding the second coming was not the same. To be able to disagree on interpretation while respecting another's point of view, is a part of what it means to be a Baptist. It is the right of a Baptist to read and understand the Bible for himself. It is a part of our priesthood.

The fact that there is no privileged class in Christianity does not, of course, forbid the setting apart of ministers or officials to perform certain specific duties for the sake of convenience and expediency in the church. Neither does it nullify the fact that God has given to his church gifted teachers and that we should avail ourselves of their ministry (Eph. 4:11-12). But it does assert the principle of individualism in religion and forbids such officials or teachers from presuming to monopolize for themselves access to God.

The Right to Freedom

Second, we are competent to make our own choices in matters of conscience. If we were created with the capacity to know God personally, it follows that we should be free to worship him without coercion or interference. And if religion is a personal matter between the soul and God, then we must be free to exercise our faith according to the dictates of our own conscience. God never forces himself on people and neither should we.

Religious liberty, then, is the political expression of soul competency. If God gave us the capacity, then we should have the right to deal with him directly. We call the capacity to know and respond to God on our own — soul competency. We call the right to worship God according to the dictates of our own conscience — soul freedom. Soul competency and soul freedom are soul mates. It may be that soul freedom is Baptists' most cherished principle.

We Americans take religious freedom for granted. But in many places in the world today it is unknown and at one time we did not have it. It was the search for religious liberty that led John Smyth and Thomas Helwys to flee England and go to Holland. It was a quest for religious liberty that led Roger Williams, a Baptist, to America. When he found no religious liberty in the colonies he fled to the wilderness and lived among the Indians. Then he founded Providence Plantation, which is now the state of Rhode Island, and there, for the first time, religious liberty was made available in America. It was a desire for religious liberty that led to the establishment of the first Baptist church in the south. And it was a demand for religious liberty by the Baptists of Virginia that led to the First Amendment — the Bill of Rights — to our Constitution that guaranteed that freedom. For 300 years Baptists have been at the forefront of the fight to protect our God-given right to religious liberty.

But if we are to be assured of religious liberty there must be a separation of church and state. Whenever and wherever there has been a union of church and state, it has inevitably resulted in the loss of religious liberty. Immediately after his conversion the apostle Paul went to the city of Damascus where he began to preach in the synagogues that Christ was the son of God. The impact of his preaching was so great that the Jewish leaders took counsel to kill him. Paul records, "In Damascus the governor under Aretas the king kept the city of Damascus with a garrison, desirous to apprehend me: and through a window in a basket was I let down by the wall, and escaped his hands" (Acts 9:24; 2 Cor. 11:32-33).

What was Paul's crime? Preaching the gospel. How did the unbelieving Jews who opposed the gospel seek to stop him? They enlisted the help of the civil authorities to accomplish their religious purposes. They sought to deny religious liberty to those with whom they disagreed. That's the principal danger of a union between church and state.

When the two are united, the powers of the state can be used to favor one religion over another. It can use its power to tax to force people to support a religion they may not believe in. It can use the power of state to impose its beliefs and practices on others, as well as suppress those who hold different beliefs.

We Baptists are committed to free churches, free synagogues, free temples and free mosques — where all persons are free to practice their faith without governmental interference or favor. And we are committed to a free state — where government is never used to force the God of the majority on the consciences of the minority. Our forefathers built a wall of separation between church and state and we are determined to help guard it.

While we believe in the separation of church and state, we don't believe in the separation of church and statesmen. Christians ought to seek public office and seek to bring the highest values possible into society. But we should never seek to promote our faith by political power. We should never seek government aid for the support of religion. Public money should be used only for public purposes. And we should never attempt to hinder another from the free exercise of their religious faith.

The Right to Govern

Third, we are competent to discern God's will for ourselves in matters of the church. Equality before God gives us equal standing in the church. Thus, all believers have a right to equal privilege in the church. That makes the church a democracy. This democracy is the institutional expression of soul freedom.

I have read that Thomas Jefferson got his idea of democracy from attending a Baptist church with his grandmother. I can believe that. A Baptist church is the purest form of democracy there is.

Most Baptist churches have regular business meetings. It is one of the few places where any member can stand up and say what they think, even if they don't think.

This pattern is seen clearly in the early church. In its infancy days the church was divided over the administration of its benevolence ministry. The apostles suggested a solution: "Look ye out among yourselves and find seven men, good men, godly men, and we will appoint them over these matters" (Acts 6:3). The scriptures say this "pleased the whole multitudes . . ." and they chose the seven and set them before the apostles to be ordained. The apostles exercised leadership by making a recommendation, but they did not lord it over the church. They proposed a solution to the problem, but the church did the choosing.

Years later the church was again in a dispute, this time over the doctrine of salvation. The church met and discussed the matter thoroughly. Everyone had his say. When the decision was finally made, Luke records that it pleased the apostles and the elders, "with the whole church"

(Acts 15:22). Apparently the decision was reached by the entire congregation, not a few powerful leaders.

This kind of democracy is often cumbersome and inefficient and tedious and slow, and at times it borders on being unbearable. But it is a part of the price of freedom. It is elemental: Religious liberty starts at home. Nothing so violates the basic nature of a Baptist church as the assumption of power by a few. No board, or council, or committee, or even the convention itself can tell us what we have to believe or what we have to do. Every church is independent and self-governing.

The pastor is not the authority in the church. Some would like to be. All they want is for the people to "show up, pay up, and shut up." And the deacons are not the authority in the church, although some of them act like it. Jesus is still lord of the church and he has not delegated his crown rights to any of us. The authority resides in the congregation as they seek to live under his lordship.

Baptists are sometimes called narrow-minded. We find this strange because of our insistence upon the competency of the soul. We insist that every man shall be free to decide for himself in matters of religion. We have been champions of religious freedom, not only for ourselves but for all others. We believe a person has a right to be a Baptist, Methodist, Presbyterian, Catholic, Jew, or atheist if he so chooses.

We believe we are under divine mandate to preach the gospel to all persons as we understand it, but we endeavor to win them by persuasion, not to force or coerce them. So, in reality, Baptists are the most broadminded of all people. They grant to all people the right to believe as they will. The moment we seek to coerce any person into religious beliefs we violate our own basic Baptist beliefs. We have been champions of religious freedom, not only for ourselves but for other people.

I once read, "What's the use of having pull if you don't pull?" So, I ask, what is the good of soul competency if you do not exercise it by coming to the Savior? The greatest of all privileges and rights is yours. You are free to come to God personally, individually, through faith in Jesus Christ. So do it.

Chapter 10

Religious Liberty: Born Free

Acts 22:24-28, Galatians 5:1

Years after he launched his missionary work, the apostle Paul returned to the temple in Jerusalem to worship. His presence created an uproar among the Jewish leaders and the Roman military police stepped in to prevent a riot. They arrested Paul and were about to publicly whip him when he asked if it was lawful to punish a Roman citizen without a trial. The centurion in charge then asked if he was a Roman citizen. Paul replied, "Yes, I am." The centurion said, "I bought my freedom . . . how did you get yours?" Paul said, "I was born free" (Acts 22:28).

While Paul's claim that he was "born free" refers to his legal status as a Roman citizen, it is a Baptist conviction that all persons should be born free. Our founding fathers agreed. The framers of the Declaration of Independence wrote, "We hold these truths to be self-evident, that all men are created equal, endowed by their creator with certain inalienable rights, among those being life, liberty, and the pursuit of happiness."

Liberty, we believe, is a God-given right. And among the most cherished of liberties is religious liberty. Religious liberty is the belief that everyone has a right to his own religious beliefs, however eccentric, or none; and that they may practice those beliefs without hindrance privately and publicly; and may propagate them as long as the rights of others are not infringed.

Baptists, perhaps more than any other group, have stood most valiantly and consistently for this right. Robert G. Torbet, author of a comprehensive history of Baptists, wrote: "Baptists have made a unique contribution to Protestantism, for which the world is their debtor, in their consistent witness to the principle of religious liberty." But men have not always enjoyed this freedom. It was the lack of religious liberty that nailed Jesus to the cross. The religious leaders of Israel accused him of disloyalty to Rome, but Pilate, after thoroughly investigating these charges, declared, "I find no fault in this man" (Luke 23:14, John 19:4). Why then was Jesus crucified? Nonconformity to the established religion.

It was the lack of religious liberty in Israel that led early Christians in Jerusalem to be imprisoned, flogged, ridiculed, and put to death by stoning and by the sword. Their crime? Practicing and propagating their faith.

As the apostle Paul and his missionary companions moved out into the Roman world to spread the gospel, they met with resistance from Jew and Gentile alike. Both used civil power to limit religious liberty. In Damascus the unbelieving Jews enlisted the aid of the governor in an attempt to capture and kill the apostle Paul.

In Asia Minor resistance came from pagan religions who saw Christianity as a threat to their way of life. In more than one place Paul and his fellow missionaries were beaten, imprisoned, and driven out of town. Why? For preaching and teaching the simple faith of Jesus Christ. This was the plight of the church for the first 300 years of its existence.

Church and State United

A major change took place in 312 A.D. when Constantine, emperor of the Roman empire, was converted to Christianity. The night before he was to go into a crucial battle he claimed to have seen a flaming cross and heard a voice from heaven saying, "By this sign conquer." He was victorious in battle and thus declared Christianity the official religion of the Roman empire. At the time his reign appeared to be one of the faith's greatest triumphs. The emperor now used state funds to build churches and sponsor theological conferences, rather than persecuting Christians for not worshipping him. Sadly, the triumph did not come without cost for it created union between church and state that would endure for 1200-1500 years.

As everyone has heard, "If power corrupts, absolute power corrupts absolutely." With the union of church and state, civil powers and ecclesiastical powers were blended together. As a result when the emperor was strong the church became a department of the state, and when the hierarchy was strong the state became a tool of the church.

In time, the state became subservient to the church because the church, it was believed, had power over the souls of men. With both ecclesiastical and civil power, the church became increasingly corrupt and secular. In time, the simple faith of Christ all but faded from the earth. The selling of indulgences — forgiveness for sins — sold for a price and in advance became a common practice in the church. In effect, sins were price-tagged and the souls of men were bought and sold daily.

Periodically there were dissenters who wanted to purify the church, but nonconformists were persecuted and martyred. When both civil and religious authority are in the hands of one, it can use its power to accomplish whatever it pleases.

Reform in Europe

In the 1400s and 1500's resistance to the corruption of the church sprang up on many fronts. Jan Hus, Martin Luther, John Calvin, Ulrich Zwingli, and other mighty leaders saw the inconsistencies and corruption of the church and sought to reform it.

While all of these leaders broke with Rome, and made great strides at restoring New Testament Christianity, their efforts were sadly incomplete. They all retained the doctrine of infant baptism and a state church. In Zurich, Switzerland, where Zwingli ministered, there stands a statue in his honor in which he holds a Bible in one hand and a sword in the other. It is a symbol of the union between church and state. The same statue might have been raised to Luther in Germany, Calvin in Geneva, John Knox in Scotland, or Henry VIII in England. For these mighty reformers turned out to be persecutors like the papacy before them.

Luther unloosed the dogs of persecution against the struggling and faithful Anabaptists. Calvin burned people at the stake. Zwingli had people drowned. And in England they rotted in prison.

The purest form of the reformation began in Switzerland among a group called Anabaptists. They were a despised and feared group often accused of blasphemy and sedition by Catholics and Reformers alike. They were called Anabaptists because they insisted on believers' baptism. They baptized those who had been previously baptized as infants. They rejected the name, however, because they didn't consider infant baptism valid, so they didn't consider that they were rebaptizing people. To them adult baptism was the first and not a rebaptism. Nonetheless they obtained the derogatory name of Anabaptists.

Two of the most able Anabaptist leaders were Conrad Grebel and Felix Manz. The two of them went from house to house, preaching and exhorting in their new-found faith. Together they baptized hundreds of converts.

Alarmed at the spread of Anabaptist heresy, Zurich authorities arrested Grebel and Manz, and sentenced them to life imprisonment. At the same time an ordinance was passed that prescribed death for anyone performing baptism outside the established church.

Through the help of friends, Grebel and Manz escaped and immediately took up the task of evangelism again. Grebel soon died and Manz was recaptured and sentenced to death by drowning. On January 25, 1527, he was tied to the end of a long pole and submerged in the water of Zurichzee for a time, then brought above the surface. When revived, he was asked if he would recant and thus save his life. Each time his answer was, "No! I will be true to my belief." And each time he was brought up his mother, standing on the bank, called out to him, "Felix! Do not recant! Do not recant!"

Manz was the first of thousands to be martyred for the Anabaptist cause. His crime? Nothing more than trying to be true to his conscience and propagate what he believed to be the true faith.

Struggle In England

The Reformation leapt across the English Channel and in the 1500s and 1600s England became the seed bed of discontent. There, Baptists, at least by that name, first emerged. John Smyth was a well-educated and deeply spiritual minister of the Church of England. He, in 1606, after careful study of the New Testament and after years of spiritual conflict, concluded that the Church of England was non-scriptural, and departed from it. He soon assumed leadership of a Separatists company in Gainsboro, England, along with Thomas Helwys and John Murton. King James I (1603-1625), determined to keep his promise to drive all dissenters from the land, cracked down on non-conformists and the embattled congregation fled England for Holland. There Smyth baptized himself and then baptized the other members of the congregation. Thus, to our knowledge, the first Baptist church in history was born.

In time, Helwys assumed leadership of the group and he and some of his fellow believers decided, despite the danger, to return to England to bear witness to their new faith. They believed they had no right to be refugees from their own land, and decided to go home.

In anticipation of their return, Helwys wrote a powerful work entitled, *A Short Declaration of the Mystery of Iniquity*. His book asserted the doctrine of full religious liberty — the first time such a view had been published in England. He dedicated the book to King James I, sovereign, with the blunt reminder that the king was not God, but was a man, and that God alone had authority over the souls of men. For his courage Helwys was imprisoned and left to silently and privately waste away. He died in the infamous Newgate prison in 1616.

Under various acts passed by Parliament, Baptists and other dissenters were excluded from holding public office, were required to attend services at the Anglican church and were forbidden from preaching without a license. But despite persecution and harassment, early Baptist preachers and writers continued to boldly demand liberty of conscience for themselves and for all others. In the tumultuous years that followed it was estimated as many as 3,000 dissenters died in jail under King James I and his son, Charles I.

God Bless America

It was during this difficult time that our pilgrim fathers fled England for America, many of them seeking religious liberty. The wharves of England were crowded with some of her best men and women, who counted conscience more important than convenience. Among them was Roger Williams, a brilliant, conscientious, and scholarly ordained Anglican priest, who is considered the father of religious liberty in America.

Once in America he and others did not find the religious liberty they had expected. The new colonies allowed for religious liberty, but only for the established church.

Williams was an independent thinker. Having rejected an ecclesiastical tyranny in old England, he was unwilling to submit to one in new England. So he began to argue for absolute separation of church and state and freedom of conscience. He denied that colonial authorities had jurisdiction over a man's relationship to God.

For his stand he was banished from Massachusetts Bay Colony in the winter of 1636. His flight took him to the wilderness where he took shelter among the Indians for two years. In 1639 Williams and eleven others moved to what is now Providence, Rhode Island, and formed the first Baptist church in America. Later he would secure a charter from King Charles II for Providence Plantation, where for the first time in America, complete religious liberty would be allowed.

John Clark was another champion of religious liberty in America. He arrived in Boston from England to find religious persecution in full swing. Identifying with the dissenters, he was soon a leader. He and some of his group sought out Williams, who helped them purchase a tract of land from the Indians and organized a colony in what is now Newport, Rhode Island.

They then formed the first Baptist church of Newport, the second Baptist church on American soil. Clark became a minister and continued as pastor and leader until his death in 1776.

In the summer of 1651, Clark, his faithful deacon, Obadiah Holmes, and John Crandall, went to Lynn, near Boston, to visit an aged and blind Baptist friend, William Witter. The men walked the 80 mile distance in two days and arrived at Witter's home on Saturday night. They stayed overnight with the blind friend and led a private religious service in his home on Sunday morning. While Clark was preaching, two officers interrupted the service and arrested him and his friends.

The offense? Holding divine services without the consent of the established congregational church. The three were ordered to be taken to the afternoon worship in the established church in order to cleanse their souls in the matter of worship.

Determined to make an example of them, church leaders charged them with denying the saving power of infant baptism and thus they were soul murderers. This offense, declared the prosecution, deserved capital punishment just as did any other type of murder.

The judge agreed with the prosecution, but decided to let them off with a fine. And, if they did not pay the fine and leave the colony at once, they would be "well whipt."

Friends paid the fines for Clark and Crandall, but Holmes, for conscience sake, chose the whipping. "Agreeing to the payment of my fine would constitute admission of wrong-doing," he stubbornly maintained.

The streets of Boston from the jail to the public whipping post were lined with spectators. As he was being stripped to the waist, Holmes preached a brief sermon to the crowd of onlookers, exhorting them to remain faithful to their beliefs.

Each of the 30 strokes with a whip of three hard-leather lashes, cut deep gashes through the skin. So severe was the beating that for 20 days and nights Holmes could sleep only by lying on his stomach or propped up on his knees and elbows.

Another sufferer for conscience was Henry Dunster, considered the first president of Harvard University. In 1653, upon the birth of his fourth child, he publicly announced his belief that infants should not be baptized, but that this right should be reserved for believers only. For this conviction he was deposed from office and banished from the colony. He died in want and disrepute in 1659.

It was soon after this that Williams and Clark secured a charter for Providence Plantation that brought religious freedom to America for the first time.

In the south things were not much better. Virginia was very inhospitable to dissenters. The Church of England had been established there as early as 1619 and there were severe penalties for nonconformity. Dissenters were harassed by clergy and magistrates alike. Virginia law required everyone to pay taxes to support the state church, to attend worship at the established church, to have their babies baptized, and no one could preach without a license.

But Baptists refused to do these things as a matter of conscience. And they did not believe a man needed any mandate to preach except the mantle of the Holy Spirit. Mobs armed with clubs, whips, and sticks often dragged them from the platform by the hair of their head as they preached, and they were often imprisoned, beaten, and accused of disturbing the peace. Persecutions would have stopped if they had ceased preaching, but they would not stop preaching until they stopped breathing.

The first recorded attempts in Virginia to suppress preachers by legal process was taken against Lewis Craig for preaching without a license. "I thank you, gentlemen, for the honor you did me," said Craig to the grand jury that indicted him. "While I was wicked and injurious, you took no note of me. But now, having altered my course of life and endeavoring to reform my neighbors, you concern yourselves much about me."

Craig's remarks struck the heart of "Swearing Jack" Waller, one of the jury, notorious as a gambler, for his profanity and for his fury toward the Baptists. He began to consider the absurdity of his conduct in opposing the righteous and good by law and by his own practice. He was baptized in 1767 and the next year was himself indicted for preaching.

June 4, 1768, John Waller and four of his friends were arrested and arraigned as disturbers of the peace. Waller made their defense so effectively that the magistrates offered to release them if they would promise to preach no more in the county for a year and a day. But Waller and two others refused and they were sent to jail.

While in prison they preached constantly through the bars to the people who flocked to the jail windows to hear them. They were kept in jail 43 days and then discharged without any conditions. After their discharge, Waller and his companions in the ministry resumed their labors with redoubled vigor, gathering fortitude from their sufferings and "thanking God that they were counted worthy to suffer for Christ and his gospel."

Among those persecuted for preaching was James Ireland. An immigrant from Scotland, he felt the call to preach to his Virginia neighbors in the year 1769. But the authorities ordered him to desist. Ireland later wrote, "I sat down and counted the cost, freedom or confinement, liberty or prison? Having ventured all upon Christ, I determined to suffer all for him."

When his congregation next assembled and Ireland stepped before them to preach, the constable promptly arrested him. The magistrates sentenced him to prison. His treatment there was vividly described by historian Joseph M. Dawson: "The jailer, seeing the fondness of the people for the preacher, collected four shillings and eight pence from those eager to visit him. Despite weakening from cold and improper food, he preached through the bars of the small iron gate. A plot to blow up the jail was uncovered. A physician rescued him from attempted poisoning. His tormentors burned pods of Indian pepper to smoke him to death. Yet the sturdy Scot maintained composure, continued his witness, and wrote letters to friends, headed, 'From my palace in Culpepper.'"

Build Us a Wall

Baptists knew from their long history if they were to have religious liberty a wall of separation must be built between the church and the state. A wall that would guarantee that civil authorities would never again interfere in matters of conscience. They would need it written into law.

The American Revolution was soon in full swing and Baptists joined in the fight in great numbers. They wanted freedom from the oppression of England and freedom from the oppression of their own civil authorities. When the federal Constitution was drafted in 1787 in Philadelphia, it did not contain a list of basic rights of citizens. When it was sent to the individual colonies for ratification, those who opposed it on various grounds argued that it was defective.

Baptists were among those who were disappointed. The proposed Constitution did not contain language strong enough to safeguard religious freedom, and so they voiced their concerns. James Madison of Virginia was one of the principle architects of the Constitution. When opposition to ratification began to mount, he returned home to explain and defend it. He also decided he ought to run for election as a delegate to the convention from Orange County. John Leland, a Baptist preacher and well known for his efforts to eliminate the state church in Virginia and for his vigorous support of religious freedom, was his main opponent.

The two men met to discuss at length the shortcomings of the Constitution. Madison convinced Leland that the Constitution should be ratified and that Leland's objection concerning religious liberty safeguards would be dealt with in due course. With this assurance, Leland withdrew as a candidate and he and his fellow Baptists supported Madison as a delegate, and he was elected.

In May 1789, shortly after the first Congress convened, Madison gave notice to the House of Representatives, where he served as a member, that he intended to bring up the subject of amendments to the Constitution. The result was the Bill of Rights as the first ten amendments to the U.S. Constitution. And, the first of those rights said "Congress shall make no laws respecting an establishment of religion, or prohibiting the free exercise thereof."

Free At Last

The First Amendment was designed to limit the state. The people who drew the Constitution were highly aware of original sin. That means, in essence, don't trust anybody. Religious liberty couldn't be left to chance. It had to be written into law. Now, for the first time in America, all people were guaranteed religious liberty. And people could finally say, in the immortal words of Martin Luther King, "Free at last, free at last, thank God Almighty, we're free at last."

What does freedom of religion mean to you and me?

- It means that we are free to believe in God or not believe, to accept or reject the gospel. We have freedom of religion, for religion, and from religion. A person may be a Christian or a Jew, a Moslem or an atheist without fear of reprisal.

- It means we are free to worship according to the dictates of our own conscience. No one can compel us to worship and no one can forbid us from worship. The choice is ours.

- It means we are free to support only the religions we believe in. We cannot be taxed to support a church we do not agree with. Tax money is not be used to support religious institutions. Tax money is to be used only for public purposes. Wise old Benjamin Franklin put it best, "I judge the difference between a good religion and a bad one — it is that a bad one needs the government to prop it up. A good one has God."

- It means we are free to preach and teach, to evangelize, and propagate our faith. The fight for religious freedom has been, in part, a fight for evangelism.

For these freedoms people have suffered and bled and died. For them we must now live and serve. They cost too much to not use. From every church in the land, then, let this mighty chorus go up:

My country 'tis of thee,
Sweet land of liberty,
Of thee I sing:
Land where my fathers died,
Land of the pilgrims' pride,
From every mountain side
Let freedom ring.

The
Officers
of the
Church

Chapter 11

The Pastor —
God's Gift to the Church

Eph. 4:7-13

An Englishman said to his rector, "If I should have an idiot son I think I would put him into the clergy." The quick-witted minister replied, "Evidently your father didn't agree with you."

It is the judgment of much of the world that the ministry is irrelevant and insipid. And, in its judgment, the influence of the pulpit has long since been rejected by thinking people.

But the judgment of God is quite different. The scriptures make it clear that the office of pastor is valued to God. The apostle Paul spoke of the importance of the pastor in Eph. 4:7-8, 11-13.

In these verses Paul is talking about the ascension gifts of Christ. These gifts, bestowed by Christ upon his churches after his ascension into heaven, are based upon his victory over Satan, sin, and the grave.

He has a most unusual way of describing these gifts. Everywhere else these gifts are bestowed by the Holy Spirit. Here they are bestowed by Christ himself. Everywhere else the gifts are bestowed upon individuals. Here they are bestowed upon the church as a whole. Everywhere else these gifts are endowments and abilities. Here they are people. Thus, Paul says, the greatest gifts of our Lord to his church are his gifted leaders.

He then names four specific leaders God has given to his church. First, there were apostles. The word "apostle" literally means "one who is sent." In that general sense it could refer to anyone sent out to do God's work. But technically it refers to the original twelve who accompanied Jesus during his earthly ministry. In that sense the office of apostle ceased to be when the last of the twelve died.

Second, there were prophets. The prophets were inspired preachers. They were men who, before the New Testament was written, got their message by direct inspiration from God. Since the completion of the New Testament, however, we get our message from the inspired word of God and not by direct inspiration. In that sense, the office of prophet has also passed away.

In fact, today we should beware of anyone who claims God has spoken to him. Ole Anderson, founder of the Trinity Foundation, a religious watchdog organization, put it best: "If someone tells you God told them to do something, don't believe them . . . Jesus was God's only son and he only talked to him three times in his whole life."

Third, there are evangelists. The word "evangelist" means "a bringer of good news." These were itinerant preachers who traveled from place to place establishing churches. They were the rank and file missionaries of their day. They preached the gospel in places it had not yet been preached. The office of evangelist in that sense is still operative.

The fourth office is that of pastor-teacher. The conjunction "and" is not found in the original, so he describes pastors who are teachers. The word "pastor" means "a shepherd, one who tends the flock." These were men who presided over a local congregation, feeding it and tending to its every need.

These gifted leaders, then, are God's gift to his church. The riches of the church are not found in monumental buildings and monetary investments, but in the people God has called and given to be the ministers of his redeeming grace.

In this chapter we will focus on the office of pastor-teacher. There are three words used in the New Testament for this one office. They are the words bishop, elder, and shepherd. The word "bishop" means "an overseer" or "superintendent." The word "elder" refers to a person who is older in years, and thus a person to be looked up to, worthy of respect. And the word "shepherd" refers to one who tends the flock.

Some people think these three words refer to three different offices. They believe the pastor ministers to the local congregation. They believe the elders rule over the church. And, above the elders, is the bishop who presides over a group of churches.

But this is not the case. The three words do not refer

to three different offices; rather they refer to three aspects of the same office. We know this because there are several passages in the Bible where all three words are used interchangeably to refer to the same people.

In one of these passages Luke records, "And from Miletus he (Paul) sent to Ephesus, and called the elders of the church and when they were come to him, he said to them . . . take heed therefore unto yourselves, and to all the flock, over the which the Holy Ghost hath made you overseers (literally, superintendents, bishops), to feed (literally, to tend as a shepherd) the church of God" (Acts 20:17-18, 28).

And Peter writes, "The elders which are among you I exhort, who am also an elder, and a witness of the sufferings of Christ, and also a partaker of the glory that shall be revealed: Feed (literally, to tend as a shepherd) the flock of God which is among you, taking the oversight (literally, to supervise) thereof (1 Peter 5:1-4).

In both passages the church leaders are addressed as "elders." In the Acts passage they are told the Lord had made them "overseers" and in the Peter passage, they are admonished to give "oversight" to the church. And, in both passages the elders are told to "feed" the flock, which is the work of a shepherd.

So, clearly, all three words describe one office. And the ideal pastor is all three. He is a bishop, an elder, and a shepherd.

The word bishop suggests the duty of the pastor. The word elder suggests the dignity of the pastor. The word shepherd suggests the disposition of the pastor.

The word bishop speaks of his administration of the

church; the word elder speaks of his reputation in the church; and the word shepherd speaks of his association with the church.

As bishops, we are to be men of responsibility; as elders we are to be men of credibility; as shepherds we are to be men of accessibility. Together they define the role of the pastor for us.

- The pastor is to superintend the work of God.
- The pastor is to exemplify the life of God.
- The pastor is to shepherd the people of God.

The Responsibility of the Pastor

First, the pastor, as a bishop, is to superintend the work of God. Over the years, churches I pastored went through several major building programs. On each project there was an overseer, a construction superintendent. As you know, it was not the responsibility of the superintendent to do all the work. It was his job to see that the work was done. He did not lay the bricks. He rather saw to it that the brick layers were there when they were needed and that they did their job correctly. He did not do the electrical work. He saw that it was done by having the electricians on the job when they were needed and supervised their work to see that it was done according to specifications.

Just so, it is not the responsibility of the pastor to do all the work of God. It is rather his responsibility to see that it is done. The pastor is not to make every hospital call, every prospect visit, teach every class or dry every tear. And if he tries he will not only wear himself out, he will be failing in his basic responsibility. It is the responsibility of the pastor to enlist, train, assign, and inspire others to do the work of God as he works alongside them.

The apostle Paul underscores this basic responsibility when he writes that the Lord gave the church pastor-teachers ". . . for the perfecting of the saints, for the work of the ministry, for the edifying of the body of Christ" (Eph. 4:12).

The word "perfect" is a fisherman's term. It means to "mend a net" to make it fit for use. When you fish with a net, there is always the danger of snagging it on something and tearing holes in it. A torn net will not function properly. The tear allows the fish to filter through and escape. So a fisherman's net must periodically be mended to make it fit for use.

Just so, the faithful pastor is to train and equip his people to "do the work of the ministry" and to "build up the body of Christ." He is to equip all his people to be a part of a great gospel net that sweeps over the whole community to draw people to Jesus Christ.

And, he is to keep doing this, ". . . till we all come in the unity of the faith, and of the knowledge of the son of God, unto a perfect man, unto the measure of the stature of the fullness of Christ" (Eph. 4:13).

The goal of the Christian life is for us to become like Jesus Christ. And we can never do that by simply sitting in a church pew. Jesus said he came not to be ministered unto, but to minister and to give his life a ransom for many. So if we are to grow to be like Christ, we also must reach out to others in Christian service. It is the role and responsibility of the pastor to equip his people to do this.

The responsibility to superintend the church originally had reference only to the ministry of the church. It had to refer to that because churches had no buildings, budgets, or programs in its infancy. But I believe in our day it also refers to the administration of the church.

Running a church is not all that different from running a business, a school, or an athletic team. Someone has to be in charge. Have the final say. Someone must supervise the staff, the maintenance of the buildings and grounds, the management of the budget, and the programs of the church.

Our churches are dying for a lack of this kind of supervision. Pastors need to be called, empowered, and held accountable for the supervision of the church.

I'm not suggesting that the pastor be a tin-horn dictator or a petty tyrant. But someone has to be in charge and the pastor is that person. He is to be God's overseer.

The Credibility of the Pastor

Second, the pastor, as an elder, is to exemplify the life of God. The word "elder" refers to one who is older in years and thus respected for his maturity. It suggests that the pastor is to be the kind of person people can respect, admire, look up to, and follow.

Somebody has said the difference between a prophet and a pastor is, "the prophet pops in, pops off, and pops out," while the pastor stays and gives credibility to his message by the life he lives.

Living the good life is essential to being a good pastor. Vance Havner put it this way, "God is on the lookout today for a man who will be quiet enough to get his message from God, brave enough to preach it, and honest enough to live it."

The behavior of some preachers is shameful. They cheat the government, they engage in immoral acts. And, as if that weren't enough, it's downright embarrassing the way some of them carry on in front of the church or in large auditoriums. They sweat and strut and shout and act as if they know everything there is to know about God. You just know that a lot of it is a scam. They are just trying to shake down people for money.

The scriptures are clear concerning a minister's conduct. The apostle Paul writes, "For a pastor must be a good man whose life cannot be spoken against. He must have only one wife, and he must be hard working and thoughtful, orderly and full of good deeds. He must enjoy having guests in his home and must be a good Bible teacher. He must not be a drinker or quarrelsome. But he must be gentle and kind and not be one who loves money. He must have a well-behaved family, with children who obey quickly and quietly. For if a man can't make his own family behave, how can he help the whole church?

"A pastor must not be a new Christian, because he might be proud of being chosen so soon and pride comes before a fall (Satan's downfall is an example). Also, he must be well spoken of by people outside the church — those who aren't Christians, so that Satan can't trap him with any accusations and leave him without freedom to lead his flock" (1 Tim. 3:1-7, *The Living Bible*).

A college student made a profession of faith one Sunday morning during the invitation. The pastor liked to recognize the ones who influenced people to make decisions for Christ, so he asked the young student who influenced him to become a Christian. The college student said to the pastor, "You did." The pastor knew the young man, but had never talked to him. His perplexity evaporated when the young man explained, "I listened to you preach on Sunday and I watched you live during the week and the two matched!"

The pastor is to have credibility as well as accountability. General Norman Schwarzkopf said, "Leadership is a potent combination of strategy and character. If you must be without one, choose character."

The Availability of the Pastor

Third, the pastor, as a shepherd, is to care for the people of God. The word "shepherd" literally means "to feed" and suggests the pastor's relationship to and care of his people. He is to be tender and loving toward them.

David said, "The Lord is my shepherd . . . he makes me to lie down in green pastures . . . he leads me beside the still waters . . ." (Ps. 23). And Jesus said, "I am the good shepherd: the good shepherd giveth his life for his sheep" (John 10:11). And Peter refers to Jesus as "the chief shepherd" (1 Peter 5:4).

The local church pastor, then, is an undershepherd who tends the Lord's flock under the Lord's supervision. Just as God leads and feeds us, and just as Jesus gave his life for us, the pastor is to lead the flock and feed the flock and bleed for the flock. As Christ laid down his life for us so the pastor is to lay down his life for his people. He cannot do it vicariously as Jesus did, but he can lay down his life in service and ministry.

Some pastors act as though they don't like people. They have unlisted phone numbers, don't keep office hours, don't make hospital calls, or do weddings or funerals. All they want to do is study and preach. Fred Smith, Sr., said, "I know a preacher who doesn't like people. He likes listeners and donors."

The shepherd must be among his sheep if he is to know of their needs. The same thing is necessary to be a good pastor. He must mix and mingle with the misery of the masses if he is to minister to them. It's a job requirement.

The poet expressed it this way:

> *A local pastor of great*
> *Austerity*
> *Climbed up in his high church*
> *Steeple*
> *To hear God, that he*
> *Might hand*
> *God's word down to the*
> *People.*
>
> *In his day God said, "Come*
> *Down and die."*
> *And he replied from his*
> *Steeple*
> *"Where art thou, Lord?" and*
> *The Lord replied,*
> *"Down here among my people.*

To be a good shepherd the minister must know three things. First of all, a preacher must know God. Listen to a pastor talk, listen to him preach — who does he talk about? What does he preach about? It is not enough for a minister to have an intense interest in religion and spiritual things. He must know that God is real. He must have faith in God. He must be overwhelmed by the presence of God. And Jesus Christ must be the center of his message, because Jesus Christ must be the center of his life.

A psychiatrist told a preacher friend that he would go back to church only when they started talking about God again. The preacher asked the psychiatrist what they talked about when he went to church. He responded, "Oh, I hear advice on how to be friendly, how to vote, how to have a happy marriage, how to feel better about myself. It's all good advice, but it's not different from the advice I get anywhere else. I don't think I need more advice; certainly I don't need more information; rarely do I know what to do with more exhortation — I can't get it out of my head that I need God." (William Willmon, *The Bible: A Sustaining Presence in Worship*, Valley Forge, Judson Press, 1981, page 33.)

Second, the preacher must know the Bible. The Bible, and the Bible alone, must be the source of his message."Preach the word" — that's what the apostle Paul said, and so far as we are concerned today, that means, "Preach the Bible."

Maybe the preacher is a psychologist or a literary scholar, or an artist. But that is not enough. When he preaches there is only one thing you need to hear, and that is the message that comes from the Bible, the message that comes from God. The only kind of preacher who can really help you is one who preaches the Bible.

It is the Bible that reveals the salvation of God accomplished through the death and resurrection of Jesus Christ. It is the Bible that reveals how we should live our lives in relationship to God and others. It is the Bible that summons us to purity and joy and peace. It is the Bible that fills our hearts with the hope of eternal life. It is the Bible that prepares us for entrance into glory. Who could want anything more? The preacher who fails to bring his people the one message that can truly change them, neglects his most sacred duty.

Finally, he must know people. Preachers don't preach in a vacuum; they preach to people who have real needs. And preachers must know and understand those needs to be effective in communicating God's word to them.

One of the great preachers of all time, John Calvin, spoke directly to people's needs, and one reason for this was that he had all the same needs himself. There were times when he didn't have enough money; his only son died in infancy; he was disgraced by a family member; one of his closest colleagues deserted the faith; his health was precarious. When you read a list of his ailments, you wonder how he survived and did any preaching at all. He knew the agony and the ecstasy of the human condition because he himself lived fully. He preached directly to people's needs because he himself had been strengthened by God and the Bible in his own time of need.

So, for a preacher to be effective he must know God,

know the Bible, and know human life well enough to be able to sympathize with the experiences of his people.

While a minister is to correct and to rebuke, he is also to encourage. All three must be done with great tenderness and patience. A good shepherd doesn't delight in beating up on his sheep. Billy Sol Estes, a wheeling, dealing, Texas businessman who wound up in prison because of his shady practices, once said, "You can shear a sheep every year, you can't skin him but once." Pastors need to remember that.

I was preaching at the First Baptist Church of Wetumpka, Alabama. On the desk of the pastor was his nameplate, "Dr. Charles Hobson — kisser of frogs." I thought, "That's the mission of every pastor, to turn frogs into princes." They are to be encouragers. They are to build up the body. They are to strengthen people.

Bishops, elders, shepherds, that's what pastors are to be. They are to superintend the work of God, exemplify the life of God, and shepherd the people of God.

When they do that, they are truly God's gift to his church.

CASE FOR DEACONS — Acts 6:1 —

Characterists FOR DEACONS — I Tim 3:8 fp

CLIMAX FOR DEACONS — Acts 6:7

Chapter 12

Deacons —
The Special Servants
of the Church

Acts 6:1-7

In one of my early pastorates I had a deacon friend, Jack Majors, who was a member of another congregation in the city. His church had an annual homecoming and it was their practice to have an active deacon give a testimony about a deceased deacon who had been a special blessing to him and to the church. That year, the responsibility of giving the testimony had fallen to Jack.

One evening, as he sat at the supper table and thought about his assignment, he asked his wife, "Honey, who are some of our dead deacons?" She quipped back, "Well, you Jack, are, for one."

Brian Harbour, pastor of First Baptist Church, Richardson, Texas, told me one Sunday a staff member met little Susan in the hall following Sunday School. He asked her, "Susan, what did you learn in Sunday School today?" Susan replied, "We learned how to heal the sick and cast out deacons."

Some people think that wouldn't be a bad idea. To them deacons are just a group of men who are over the hill and who keep the pastor over the barrel.

The fact is, the office of deacon is a high and holy one. It is one of only two chosen offices in the New Testament church. The scriptures make this clear in two places. In Philippians 1:1, as the apostle Paul addressed the church, he mentioned three distinct groups of people: saints, bishops, and deacons. Saints were the rank and file church members. Bishops and deacons were the chosen officers of the church.

And in 1 Timothy 3:1-13 the apostle Paul set out the qualifications of these same two officers, because they were the only two officers in the church — bishops and deacons. Bishops, as we have already seen, were the "overseer" or "superintendent" of the church. And deacons were the special servants of the church.

The emphasis of this passage is on what both the pastor and deacon are to be, rather than on what they are to do. That's because being always comes before doing. Both bishops and deacons are always to be men of God, people of character, right with God, their family, and their fellow men in every way. But, what they are to do may vary from time to time and place to place, depending on the need of the church. But if they are what they are supposed to be, you can be sure they will do what they are supposed to do.

To better understand what a deacon is to do, why they are needed, we need to look at the origin of the office. A record of this beginning is given in Acts 6:1-7. Following Pentecost, the New Testament church experienced a time of dynamic growth. Those first disciples who had been with Jesus knew of his "purse" from which he gave support to the poor (John 12:6; 13:29) and they quickly took up the same practice. So from the beginning the New Testament church was involved in the social ministry of supporting widows, a work largely handled by the apostles themselves.

But the church was exploding in membership and this posed grave problems within itself. With its unprecedented growth, it was not keeping pace organizationally and administratively. Too many things were slipping through administrative cracks.

Among them was adequate care for all the widows. There were two distinct groups of widows in the church — Greeks and Hebrews. The Grecian widows were Jews who lived beyond the borders of Palestine. In those faraway places they had adopted Greek customs and spoke the Greek language. The Hebrew widows on the other hand kept their old ways. The Greek widows felt they were not being fairly treated. The result was polarization over the benevolent ministry — and an unhappy, complaining congregation.

Finding themselves with more work than they could handle, and a murmuring membership, the apostles called the congregation together and suggested they choose from the membership seven men of good reputation, with a deep faith in God, administrative ability, and who were filled with the Holy Spirit. These, they suggested, should be appointed over the task of ministering to the poor.

Their recommendation pleased the congregation and they chose seven of their group for this work. It is remarkable that of the seven selected, every one of them had a Greek name and were Greek-speaking Jews. Obviously the church felt this was the best way to assure the Hellenistic widows of their support.

This being done, they were set before the apostles and when they had prayed, they "laid their hands on them." The laying on of hands was a formal symbol of their appointment to this duty. It was an ancient practice that symbolized the impartation of the gift of grace.

This arrangement worked well and was followed by an enormous increase in the number of believers under the apostles' preaching. The proof that harmony had been restored was that the work of God grew mightily.

Why were deacons chosen in the beginning?

- It was not an honorary office. It is an honor to be chosen a deacon, but it is not an honorary position. We don't have honorary Sunday School teachers or honorary choir members and we don't have honorary janitors, so we shouldn't have honorary deacons.

- It was not an authoritative office. They were not chosen to be a board of directors or in any way to rule the roost. It is at this point, that the office of deacon is most often misunderstood. The deacon body is sometimes referred to as "the board of deacons." The word "board" goes back to the early days of our history when the leaders of a community sat around a wooden table, called a board (as in "room and board"), and discussed issues of importance to them. But when deacons, or any large group in the church, become a board to run it, they usually become either a rubber stamp or a bottleneck, neither of which is good, nor is it scriptural.

• It is a servant office. There is absolutely nothing in the New Testament to indicate deacons were ever to have anything other than a servant capacity. In fact, that is what the word "deacon" literally means — a servant. Their original function was to serve tables and relieve the apostles for this work so that they could give themselves to prayer and preaching.

It is when the deacon is looked on in this light that the office gains its highest dignity. As Jesus taught, "Whosoever of you will be great among you shall be the servant of all" (Mark 10:44).

In the unbelieving world greatness is measured by the number of people a person rules over. The more powerful and influential an individual is, the more people there are under his control.

But, in the kingdom of God it is not so. In the Christian realm the one who is greatest is the one who serves the most. We must be careful lest we adopt in the church the world's standards and not our Lord's standards.

But, some people, reading the King James account of

the establishment of this office and in particular the phrase that these be men "whom we may appoint over this business," have argued, "See, deacons were chosen to be over the business of the church." I agree that the first deacons were chosen to be over the business of the church, so long as we realize what the real "business" of the church is. It is ministry. The first deacons were chosen to administer the benevolent program of the church in a fair and equitable manner and to thus free the apostles, devoting themselves to preaching and praying as the Lord intended. They were never intended to be a ruling body.

Where, then, did this idea of the deacons as a governing board arise? It was about 1,800 years later, when J. M. Pendleton released his *Church Manual* (1867), that the role of deacons in Southern Baptist life apparently changed dramatically. Pendleton called for deacons to be heavily involved in the business affairs of the church.

And Pendleton, the leader of the Landmark Movement, was only looking back to *The Deaconship*, authored by R. B. C. Howell in 1846. Howell, pastor of First Baptist Church, Nashville, Tennessee, wrote deacons were to serve as the financial officers of the church. This may be the first mention in Baptist history of deacons as the executive board of the church. This was a tragic step, for as Herschel H. Hobbs said, "There is no place for a boss in a Baptist church."

The church is not to be run by a board or bullied by a dictator. It is to be led by the Lord through the entire congregation voicing its will. In the beginning the apostles didn't run the church and the deacons didn't run the church. The church ran the church. The democratic process shines through here. A proposal was made. The people were pleased. And "the whole multitude" decided.

Actually it is the deacon's service and ministry that qualifies him to give administrative leadership to the church. The business of the church should never be determined on the basis of dollars and cents alone. Unless deacons are out among the people, feeling their pain and heartache, they can't know how best to spend the Lord's money, what new staff members are needed, and what programs ought to be inaugurated. For deacons to make leadership decisions without first being among the people in ministry is like a doctor trying to treat a patient he has never seen. A physician needs to feel the patient's pulse, look into the patient's eyes, check his temperature, to treat him effectively. It takes personal contact with the patient to prescribe the best cure. The same thing is true with the spiritual health of the church.

What were the results of these first deacons being elected? Needs were served; conflict was settled; the apostles were freed to focus on their primary task; and the number of believers was multiplied greatly. What happened there ought to happen in every church and in every age every time deacons are ordained. Every deacon ordination ought to result in these same things.

What were the results of this first ordination? What ought to result from the ordination of deacons today? There are three significant things:

- the unification of the church,

- the emancipation of the pastor, and
- the multiplication of disciples.

In every age and in every church the ordination of deacons ought to bring about these same results.

Where There Is Quarreling, the Devil Is There

First, the ordination of deacons ought to result in the unification of the church. In the beginning, the church that was about to be polarized was brought back to unity. The problem was inequities or perceived inequities in administering the church's benevolent program. This led to "murmuring" by the neglected widows.

Multiplication without ministry always leads to murmuring in a church. People need, and have a right, to be ministered to when they have needs. If they aren't, they will not be happy.

Complaining and division in the church have been the curse of Christianity from the beginning. Perhaps that is why Paul wrote, "Do all things without murmurings and disputings" (Phil. 2:14). The Greek word for "murmur" describes the buzzing of bees' wings when they are mad. It suggests a low, growling, guttural sound. It was under the breath, behind the back complaining. "Wrangling" is more open and direct conflict. Both have greatly hampered the work of God.

Years ago I received a letter from a pastor in Africa whom I had met on a mission trip. He wrote, "We need prayers very badly in this area. The devil is working mightily, for the first people to work in this station left the gospel and then started quarreling. And, you know, where there is quarreling the devil is there."

Need I remind you grumbling is not one of the spiritual gifts. It doesn't take much musical ability to always be harping on something. So don't go through life standing at the complaint counter. Remember the squeaking wheel doesn't always get the grease. It sometimes gets replaced.

Let people begin to quarrel and they dissipate their best energies on conflict rather than God's work. And more often than not, the problems in churches are not caused by big men wanting to serve but by little men wanting to rule. I remind you, deacons were chosen to solve problems, not create them. They were elected to serve, not rule. They were chosen to unify, not divide.

Churches need to elect capable committees, give them clear instructions on what to do, empower them to act, and then hold them accountable. That will solve lots of problems and eliminate lots of wrangling. And deacons need to minister to the needs of the congregation. These two things, as much as anything I know, could bring peace to the church.

Nibbled to Death by a Thousand Minnows

Second, the ordination of deacons ought to result in the emancipation of the pastor. As a result of the selection and ordination of these first deacons in the first church, the overworked apostles were set free to concentrate on their primary calling.

The unrest in the early church was diverting the apostles from their first duty. So they urged the congregation to elect deacons, so, as they said, "We can give ourselves continually to prayer and to the ministry of the Word."

This statement forever establishes the priority of the pastor. It is to the Word. He is "to hold Christ and his cross before the people." This is not to say that other things are not important. But, everything can't be first. Something has to have priority in our life. And the pastor's first job is to hold Christ and the cross before men.

I have already stated that one of the three words in scripture for the office of pastor is "bishop." It means "an overseer" or "a superintendent." That's what the pastor is to be. He is like a construction superintendent. He is not to do all the work of the church. He is to see to it that all the work is done. He is to train, organize, and motivate the people to do the work of the ministry.

Our churches today need a better division of labor. Most ministers and their staff are both overworked and underemployed. They are overworked at a hundred little things and underemployed at the basic calling to pray and preach and to train and equip the people for the work of the ministry.

While the prophet Jonah was swallowed by a whale, today's modern-day prophet is nibbled to death by a thousand minnows of interruption. The solution: Let the pastor be the superintendent, an overseer, and spread the work of the ministry among the members of the church, especially the deacons.

Many people, when they describe their church, say, "Our church has one minister and 500 members." What they ought to say is, "Our church has one pastor and 500 ministers." All of God's people are to be ministers, and it is the pastor's responsibility to equip them for special service.

Deacons need to see themselves as friends, helpers, and fellow servants with, not antagonists to, the pastor. One of my preacher boys called me one day and said he was having trouble with four of his deacons. These four deacons had run off the last four pastors in the church and now they were giving him trouble. He said, "What should I do? Should I square off and fight them? Should I take a baseball bat to them? How should I handle it?"

I told him to be very patient, gentle, and kind. Time takes care of a lot of things.

Sure enough, the next time I saw him he told me how things had worked out. He said one of those deacons was working in his yard one Saturday when he suddenly was struck with a heart attack and died. He said he would preach the funeral and the other three men served as pall bearers. Then, a few weeks later, a second of those deacons was driving to work when he was hit by an eighteen-wheeler and killed instantly. He said that he preached the funeral and the other two served as pall bearers.

Then, he said, the third of those men learned that he had cancer, it had spread rapidly, and within a few weeks he was dead. He said that he preached the funeral and the one remaining man assisted as a pall bearer.

Following the last funeral the remaining deacon rode with him back to the church. In their conversation he leaned over and said, "Preacher, I want you to know I have been on your side all the time."

The work of God goes forward best when pastors and

deacons see themselves as being on the same side; as serving the congregation together. One ministering primarily to the spiritual needs and the other to the physical needs.

Sam Rayburn, who was a member of the U.S. House of Representatives for 48 years, took a back seat to no one. Someone once asked him how many presidents he had served under.

"I served under no president," Rayburn corrected. "I served 'with' eight."

That's the way it should be in the church. It is not a matter of one being over the other. It is a matter of standing shoulder to shoulder, side to side, and together ministering for God.

A Fast Way of Adding

Third, the ordination of deacons should result in the multiplication of disciples. When the first deacons were chosen a stagnated church surged forward into a new period of growth and outreach.

This experience has a happy ending. As a result of the apostles and the deacons sharing the ministry of the church, harmony was restored and another evangelistic spiral resulted. Luke records, "The word of God increased; and the number of the disciples multiplied in Jerusalem greatly; and a great company of priests were obedient to the faith" (Acts 6:7).

Up until now people were simply "added" to the church. But, in this chapter, the writer begins to talk about "multiplication." (Multiplication is just a fast way to add.) This suggests a basic principle of church growth: a ministering church is a happy church, and a happy church will be a growing church. A superbly organized church and planned ministry will fail without active care, love, and service of the people towards others.

Harmony is essential to the church doing its work. No church can be effective if its members are at civil war. And the happiest churches I know are those where the ministry and leadership are shared by the pastor and the deacons.

God's plan seems clear to me: He expects his church to be a growing and ministering church. It is not only to become larger and larger, but to maintain a personal touch all the while.

How big should the church be? From a study of Acts there is apparently no limit to how large a church can be so long as it can maintain a personal ministry to all who are its members. Its size is to be limited only by the number of active, dedicated lay ministers it has.

And the deacons are the primary means of the church maintaining this personal ministry while it continues to grow.

When the pastors pray and preach and when the deacons minister, the church has an unbeatable combination for doing both. These held in balance will create peace and harmony among God's people and enable us to grow an evangelistic church that reaches, serves, and keeps people.

The
Ordinances
of the
Church

Chapter 13

Baptism: The Ordination of the Laity

Matt. 28:19-20

Never was there a person who seemed to care less about ritual and ceremony than Jesus. By practice and by teaching he emphasized a simple, direct, personal relationship with God. Born into a world where religion had been reduced to rules and rituals, he emphasized relationships.

He reduced the commands of God to two: love God with all of your being and love your neighbor as you love yourself. And he left just two rituals/ceremonies for his followers to observe — baptism and the Lord's Supper. Some have tried to add a third one, footwashing, but there is no justification for their claims in this. Christ washed his disciples' feet on one occasion to teach them the spirit of humility, but this was not given as an ordinance to memorialize any particular thing (John 13:1-15).

The importance of these two ordinances cannot be overestimated. Both center in the cross. Baptism shows what happened to Jesus when he went to the cross; the Lord's Supper shows what happens to us when we go to the cross. When Jesus went to the cross, his body was broken and his blood was shed for the sins of the world. When we go to the cross, we who are dead in sin, die to sin and we are raised to walk in a newness of life. Because these both depict the gospel, we will never outgrow our need to observe them. And, as long as we observe them in the proper manner, we will never drift from the heart of the Christian faith. So, in a sense, they are anchors to the gospel.

They are not sacraments; to call them sacraments is to vest them with a saving power which they do not have. They are memorials — monuments — given to symbolize the gospel and our salvation.

In what sense is the Lord's Supper a monument? By partaking of the broken bread, and the new wine, we do so in memory of his body that was broken for us, and his blood that was spilled for us. These are but reminders of his death. He said: "As oft as ye do this, do it in remembrance of me."

In what sense is baptism a monument? It is a monument to a historical fact — that Jesus died, that he was buried, and that he arose from the dead. These were facts in history, not just religious theories. When we are baptized we say to the world, "I believe that Jesus died, that he was buried, and that he arose from the dead."

Our baptism is also a monument to a personal experience. Charles Haddon Spurgeon said, "Christ came not to make bad men good or good men better, but to make dead men live." Baptism depicts that. Our experience is that we have died to the old life of sin and have been raised up to walk a new life, that the old life has ended and we have begun a new life.

Our baptism is also a monument to our commitment. When we were baptized we said to the world, "You may expect better things of me from this day; I am a new creature, and pledge myself to live a new life." Our baptism is a monument to preserve that pledge for all coming time.

And our baptism is also a monument to our hope of eternal life. By it we say just as Jesus was raised up from the dead, we believe that he will one day raise us up. Our baptism does not give us eternal life, but it is a public declaration of our belief in, and our hope in, eternal life.

Baptism is a simple act. It consists of taking a person into a pool of water and immersing them in the name of the Father, the Son, and the Holy Ghost. Nancy Rogers told me the story of some children who were playing church. They decided they would baptize their cat as a part of the service. So the little girl took the animal and as she dipped it in the water said, "I baptize you in the name of the Father, the Son, and into the hole you go." That's not exactly the baptismal formula, but the picture is accurate.

Should you and I be baptized? Consider this: First, Jesus himself was baptized, setting an example for us (Matt. 3:13-17). And he commanded all believers to be baptized when he said, "Go ye therefore, and teach all nations, baptizing them in the name of the Father, and of the Son, and of the Holy Ghost: teaching them to observe all things whatsoever I have commanded you: and, lo, I am with you alway, even unto the end of the world" (Matt. 28:19-20). That is why it is called an ordinance.

And the early church practiced baptizing from its beginning. After Peter's first sermon, this commentary is made, "Then they that gladly received his word were baptized" (Acts. 2:41).

Since baptism was commanded by Christ and is so prominent in the Bible, it must be important to every believer. It is, in fact, a sermon in symbols — the first sermon you will preach as a believer in Christ. That is, perhaps, why Jerome, the fourth century saint, called it "the ordination of the laity." It is a sermon with four points:

- First, it depicts what Jesus did for us. He died, was buried, and was raised again on the third day.

- Second, it depicts what Jesus has done in us. We who were dead in sin, died to sin, and have been raised to newness of life in Christ.

- Third, it depicts what Jesus will do for us. He will resurrect us from the grave at the end.

- Finally, it depicts what Jesus expects from us. That we will walk in a new kind of life.

Three things are necessary for this sermon to be preached clearly and accurately:

- Baptism must be for believers only.

- Baptism must be by immersion only.

- Baptism must be as a symbol only.

From Chickens to Ducks

First, baptism is for believers only. Nothing is clearer than this in scripture. There is no example in the Bible of anyone being baptized except a believer in Jesus Christ. Look at these verses:

- "They that gladly received his word were baptized and the same day there were added unto them about three thousand souls" (Acts 2:41).

- "But when they believed Philip preaching the things concerning the kingdom of God, and the name of Jesus Christ, they were baptized, both men and women" (Acts 8:12).

- "Then Simon himself believed also: and when he was baptized, he continued with Philip, and wondered, beholding the miracles and signs which were done" (Acts 8:13).

- "And Crispus, the chief ruler of the synagogue, believed on the Lord with all his house; and many of the Corinthians hearing believed, and were baptized" (Acts 18:8).

- "And as they went on their way, they came unto a certain water; and the eunuch said, 'See, here is water; what doth hinder me to be baptized?' And Philip said, 'If thou believest with all thine heart, thou mayest.' And he answered and said, 'I believe that Jesus Christ is the son of God' " (Acts 8:36-37).

- "And brought them out and said, 'Sirs, what must I do to be saved?' And they said, 'Believe on the Lord Jesus Christ, and thou shalt be saved, and thy house.' And they spake unto him the word of the Lord, and to all that were in his house. And he took them the same hour of the night, and washed their stripes; and was baptized, he and all his, straightway" (Acts 16:30-33).

Do you see the scriptural pattern? It is always, "Believe first, and then be baptized." Not all people believe this. Some churches practice infant baptism. But there is absolutely no scriptural reference to justify this practice, for infants do not believe.

Infant baptism does not appear in scripture at all and it is not mentioned in history until shortly before the close of the second century, when Tertullian at Carthage opposed it as an innovation. The belief that baptism was essential to salvation and that infants dying unbaptized were lost facilitated the growth of infant baptism; but no one advocated it before Augustine (354-430 A.D.).

In Chapter 7, "People of the Book," you read of the ocean voyages of Congregational missionaries Adoniram and Ann Judson and Luther Rice. Though on different vessels enroute to their mission station in India, they studied the same New Testament. All three, without conferring, became convinced that the Baptist way of believer's baptism by immersion was the proper mode. Integrity caused them to become Baptists upon reaching India.

Ann Hasseltine Judson wrote in her diary in Calcutta, India, September 1, 1812, "I have been examining the subject of baptism for some time past, and contrary to my prejudices and my wishes, am compelled to believe that believer's baptism alone is found in scripture. If ever I sought to know the truth; if ever I looked up to the father of light; if ever I gave myself to the inspired word, I have done so during this investigation . . . We expect soon to be baptized. Oh, may our hearts be prepared for that holy ordinance . . ."

The Great Awakening in America was greatly fostered by the preaching of George Whitfield, a dynamic Methodist minister. Many who were converted under Whitfield's preaching eventually became Baptists. On one occasion, as he pondered how he had helped produce many Baptists who immersed their candidates fully into the baptismal pool, he ruefully said, "All my chickens have become ducks."

According to scripture, the Lord would have all his chickens become ducks. Baptism is for believers only.

Lightning and Lightning Bugs

Second, baptism is by immersion only. Years ago a man from a denomination that practices baptism by sprinkling began visiting the church I pastored. He was seriously considering joining our church until he learned that he would have to be immersed.

He spent many hours studying to build a case for sprinkling. His conclusions were the same arguments that others have used. There was nothing new in them. But, when he was finished, he brought me an eight-page paper defending his position.

My response to him was simple: If words have mean-

ing, and that's what words are — sounds with meaning —
then immersion is the only correct way to baptize because
that's what the word baptize meant in Jesus' day.

Mark Twain once said, "The difference between the
right word and the almost right word is the difference between lightning and a lightning bug." There's that much
difference in immersion and sprinkling. Jesus said what
he meant and meant what he said.

A young man came to me once wanting to be baptized.
He had one problem. He had a broken arm and the doctor
told him he should not get the cast wet. I said, "That's all
right. We'll hold your arm out of the water as I baptize
you." He, being familiar with the scriptures, said, "No, I'll
put it in a plastic sack. I want to be put all the way under."

That's what the Lord meant when he told us to go and
be baptized. And, that's the way we ought to do it.

The Ordination of the Laity

Finally, baptism is a symbol only. It has no saving
power. It does not wash away any sins. Jerome saw in
this symbolism "the ordination of the laity." There is no
magic in the water we use. It is the same kind of water we
drink and the same kind we bathe in.

The purpose of baptism is to identify us openly and
publicly with the death, burial, and resurrection of our
Lord. Romans 6:3-5 says, "Know ye not, that so many of
us were baptized into Jesus Christ were baptized into his
death? Therefore we are buried with him by baptism into
death; that like as Christ was raised up from the dead by the
glory of the Father, even so we also should walk in newness

of life. For if we have been planted together in the likeness of death, we shall be also in the likeness of his resurrection." And Colossians 2:12 says, "Buried with him in baptism, wherein also ye are risen with him through the faith of the operation of God, who hath raised him from the dead."

Just as a wedding ring identifies us as married and a diploma identifies us as graduates, so baptism identifies us as believers. It is an open, public confession of our faith in Christ.

If baptism were necessary to our salvation, Jesus would surely have baptized people. But he didn't. John 4:1-3 says, "When therefore the Lord knew how the Pharisees had heard that Jesus made and baptized more disciples than John (though Jesus himself baptized not, but his disciples), he left Judea and departed again into Galilee."

And the apostle Paul would not have boasted that he had not baptized the people of Corinth. But he did. He said, "I thank God that I baptized none of you, but Crispus and Gaius; lest any should say that I had baptized in mine own name. And I baptized also the household of Stephanas; besides, I know not whether I baptized any other" (1 Cor. 1:14-16).

Clearly, then, baptism does not save, but it identifies us with the death, burial, and resurrection of the savior. Should you be baptized? The answer is yes. Not to become a Christian, but because you are a Christian. Joyce Kilmer wrote, "Poems are made by fools like me, but only God can make a tree." And, only God can make a Christian. But once you become a Christian you should follow the Lord in baptism as an act of obedience.

Peter spoke of it as the "answer to a clear conscience." He wrote, "The like figure whereunto even baptism doth also now save us (not the putting away of the filth of the flesh, but the answer of a good conscience toward God), by the resurrection of Jesus Christ" (1 Peter 3:21).

Peter emphasizes here that baptism is a figure and that it does not put away the filth of the flesh. But it is the answer to a good conscience toward God.

I mentioned the Judsons and Luther Rice earlier. In a letter to his parents from India dated November 2, 1812, Luther Rice wrote these words, ". . . But let conveniences be what they may, I hope nothing shall deprive me of the consolation, resulting from a conscience void of offense. Yesterday, I was baptized by the Reverend Mr. Ward, and enjoyed the privilege of uniting with the Baptist church in Calcutta, in celebrating the sacred ordinance of the Lord's supper. It was a comfortable day to my soul!"

That's baptism as the Lord intended it. What doth hinder you from being baptized?

Chapter 14

The Lord's Supper —
We Remember!
We Remember!

1 Cor. 11:23-34

There are six words written across the front of most Lord's Supper tables. I must have looked at them a thousand times, but not long ago I stopped and really focused on the words inscribed on one, "This do in remembrance of me."

Those words were first spoken by Jesus to his disciples as they were gathered around him in the upper room (Luke 22:19). They had met there to celebrate the Passover. The Passover was a Jewish festival first established by God while Israel was still in Egyptian bondage (Ex. 12:1-51). It was intended as a time of remembrance.

What was Israel to remember? They were to remember what God had done for them — God's mighty acts as he delivered them from bondage and guided them through the wilderness to the promised land.

It was at the close of the Passover that Jesus gave this command: This do in remembrance of me. All three synoptic gospels relate the account of this event (Matt. 26:26-30; Mark 14:22-26; Luke 22:14-20). But it was left to the apostle Paul to interpret the event for us. He wrote, "For I have received of the Lord that which I also delivered unto you, that the Lord Jesus the same night in which he was betrayed took bread: and when he had given thanks, he brake it, and said, Take, eat, this is my body which is broken for you: This do in remembrance of me. After the same manner he also took the cup, when he had supped, saying, This cup is the new testament in my blood: this do ye, as oft as ye do it, in remembrance of me. For as often as ye eat this bread, and drink this cup, ye do show the Lord's death till he come" (1 Cor. 11:23-26).

"This do in remembrance of me." Why do you suppose the Lord Jesus left these words with us? Because he knew how easily the human mind forgets. The Greeks had an adjective which they used to describe time — "time" they said, "wipes all things out." To them the mind was like a slate, and time a sponge which wiped it clean. Jesus was saying, "In the rush and press of things you will forget me."

These were not words just to his disciples as they gathered with him that Thursday evening. They are also words to his church today. What are we to remember? We are to remember what God has done for us in the person of Jesus Christ. To do this is not optional. It is a command. That's why we call it an ordinance.

Hans Kung set it all in perspective when he said: "Christianity exists only where the memory of Jesus Christ is advocated in theory and practice." We must not forget Christ. Remembering him is the one essential of our faith.

It was the simplest of ceremonies that he set forth to establish our remembrance of him. It consisted of gathering around a table and eating bread that symbolized his body and drinking wine that symbolized his blood. Not by tall buildings or shaft of marble, did he ask to be remembered. It was by two unchangeable customs: eating and drinking. As long as men live they must eat and drink. And these are the means he gave for keeping alive his memory.

What are we to remember? Three things in particular:

- We are to remember his death.
- We are to remember his presence.
- We are to remember his return.

Never Forget Your Sins

First, and foremost we are to remember his death. Paul wrote, "As often as ye eat this bread, and drink this cup, ye show the Lord's death till he come" (1 Cor. 11:26).

The one incident in his eventful career that Jesus selected to be preserved among all others was his death. He made his death more important than his holiness, or his wisdom, or his power, or his miracles, or his teachings.

He frequently referred to his death as the high hour of his life. He called it "mine hour," as if that were the sole purpose of his coming to earth — as if it were the one hour of his life for which all other hours existed.

Let the world forget everything else he ever taught, but

let them not forget his death. To that end he established this ordinance. He gave it to preserve unchangeably this one immutable thing — he died for every person; let this fact never be forgotten.

Malcolm Muggeridge said concerning his death, "One thing at least can be said with certainty about the crucifixion of Christ; it was manifestly the most famous death in history. No other death has aroused one-hundredth part of the interest, or been remembered with one-hundredth part of the intensity and concern."

And why did Christ select his death as the one incident in his eventful career to be preserved above all others? It was by his death that day that the gates of hell were lifted off their hinges; it was by his death that the foundations were cut from under the kingdom of evil; it was by his death that the doors of the prison house of Satan were thrown wide open; it was by his death that we are redeemed from our sins.

A minister preaching at a camp meeting said he felt the Holy Spirit moving in the service. At the conclusion of the message he gave an altar call. Three hundred people came forward. As they were kneeling in prayer, the minister said he was kneeling in front of a little boy. He asked the boy this question: "Young fellow, what brought you to this altar tonight?" The minister said the little boy looked him straight in the face and said, "My sins, sir, my sins."

That's why we all come to the cross and that's why we come to the Lord's table. Charles Clayton Morrison, perhaps the premier religious journalist of the early twentieth century, once said that the church is the only institution in the world whose membership is based on unworthiness to be a member. And, that's the basis of the good news. In Christ God came into the world to do for us what we were unable to do for ourselves, namely to create within us clean hearts of righteousness and love. God was in Christ reconciling the world to himself.

We are not perfect people. We do not gather at the Lord's table because we deserve to be there. We are recipients of grace — undeserved love! "Grace is doing for someone what they do not deserve, have not earned, could not ask for, and cannot repay."

His death is the only thing in his life he desired to memorialize. But he regarded it the most important hour of his life. It must be told around the world; it must be put in every language; let the mothers of earth tell it to their children at their knees.

He wrote no books, but more books have been written about him than about any other man who ever lived. He composed no songs, but more hymns have been written and dedicated to him than have been dedicated to any other name on earth. He built no house, but more houses have been dedicated to him than any name or cause during all the passing years. The fact that he died to save the lost, that he loved the unloved and unlovable, made his death the most monumental thing that ever occurred since the beginning of time.

That's why we do this "in remembrance" of him.

Never Overcome the Numbness

Second, we remember his presence. Our remembering of Jesus is more than a historical recollection. We are not like people at a wake for a dead man. Jesus is not some distant memory, but he is presently the reigning lord. It is a remembrance of his presence among us that we gather about his table.

There are various views on the meaning and interpretation of the Lord's Supper. Catholics believe in what they call Transubstantiation. This is the belief that when a person partakes of the supper, the Lord performs a miracle and changes the bread into the actual body of Jesus and the wine into the actual blood of Jesus.

Episcopalians and Lutherans hold to what they call Consubstantiation. This is the belief that the Holy Spirit is present with the bread and wine, and gives them unusual power of blessings. This does not go quite as far as Catholicism, but it is not far behind.

We hold that the ordinance is purely symbolic — that it is a symbol of the death, that it is a reminder of it, that it is to be kept as a memorial of the death.

There is no saving virtue either in the Lord's Supper or in baptism. They are both pictures of his death and resurrection. The whole gospel story is crowded into these two ordinances.

But, we do believe that in a spiritual sense we meet the Lord at his table. Martin Marty said it well: "The Lord's Supper is often called 'Holy Communion,' a coming together of bread and body, wine and blood, God with creatures, and believers with one another."

Following the death, burial, and resurrection of Jesus, he appeared to two disciples as they walked the road to Emmaus (Luke 24:13-32). Blinded by grief, they did not recognize him. As they expressed their despair over the crucifixion, he chided them, reminding them of the words of prophecy that had predicted both the death and resurrection of the Messiah. But still they did not recognize him.

It was only as they sat down to eat with him and as he took bread and blessed it and broke it and gave it to them, that their eyes were opened and they knew him.

And when he was gone from their midst they said one to the other, "Did not our heart burn within us, while he talked with us by the way, and while he opened to us the scriptures?" In a similar way our hearts burn with his presence as we come to his table to break bread and drink the cup.

Roy Smith tells of when he was a student in college in a little town in Kansas. His father worked in a steel mill and never made much money. Roy had a part, a leading part, in the school play, and his father wanted him to have a pair of new shoes for the performance. So, his father, from his meager salary, managed to save enough money to buy them for him.

The day before the play was to open, in fact as they were doing their final dress rehearsal, someone burst into the room and said, "Come quick, Roy, there's been an accident at the mill and your father has been hurt."

Roy rushed to the mill, but when he got there it was too late. His father had died. They buried him on a cold, windy hillside outside that little Kansas town. After the funeral was over, Roy went by the mill to pick up his father's tools. Someone had thoughtfully folded the overalls, covered up the blood, and put them in the bottom of the toolbox.

On top of the tools they had put his father's shoes — an old pair of brogans, placed upside down so that the soles were sticking up. Roy said when he opened the lid of that toolbox, the first thing he saw was his father's shoes — both of which had holes in the soles on them. They were worn clean through.

Roy said, "When I realized that my father stood on the cold, steel floor of that mill with holes in his shoes so that I could stand on the stage in new shoes, there came a numbness in my heart that I never overcame."

And, I tell you, if we ever overcome that numbness that first came upon us when we were saved, when we met the Lord, then we will lose something vital and essential. That's why we come to his table — we come to keep our memory alive. We come to meet the living Lord. We meet "in remembrance of him."

Never Forget His Promise

Finally, we are to remember his return. When we come to the table we not only look back to the cross and we not only look up to his presence, but we also look forward to his coming and final victory. Paul said, "As often as ye eat this bread, and drink this cup, you do show the Lord's death till he come" (1 Cor. 11:26).

Jesus said to his disciples, "In my father's house are many mansions: if it were not so, I would have told you. I go to prepare a place for you. If I go and prepare a place for you, I will come again, and receive you unto myself; that where I am there ye may be also" (John 14:2-3).

The world has not seen the last of Jesus. We have his word on that. He will come again.

The apostle Paul called the return of Christ "our blessed hope" (Titus 2:13). Why so? It is only when he comes again our salvation will be complete. For that reason we look for his coming. For that reason we remember.

Jesus is the center and the circumference of our faith. The poet put it well:

> *For the weariest day*
> *May Christ be your stay*
> *For the darkest night*
> *May Christ be your light*
> *For the weakest hour*
> *May Christ be your power*
> *For each moment's fall*
> *May Christ be your all.*

Without money and arms Jesus of Nazareth conquered more millions than Alexander, Caesar, Mohammed, and Napoleon; without science and learning he shed more light on things human and divine than Pasteur, Newton, and Salk; without eloquence of school he spoke more truth and wisdom than Aristotle, Plato, and Socrates.

As Philip Schaff, the well-known historian, said, "Without writing a single line, he set more pens in motion and finished more themes for more sermons, orations, discussions, works of art, learned volumes, and sweet songs of praise, than the whole army of great men of ancient and modern times. Born in a manger and crucified as a male-factor, he now controls the destinies of the civilized world and rules a spiritual empire which embraces one-third of the inhabitants of the globe."

We must work to keep our focus on him. The supper helps.

The great painter, Leonardo daVinci, was commissioned by the Duke of Milan to paint "The Last Supper." The great painter labored diligently for several years, paying careful attention to every detail of the disciples' faces, the grouping around the Lord's table, the chalice, and, of course, the face of Jesus.

Finally, it was ready for Leonardo to share the fruits of his labor with a friend. The friend was awestruck as he marveled at this beautiful work of art, and he said in wonder, "Oh, what a beautiful chalice. I can't take my eyes off it." Leonardo immediately took his brush and painted through the chalice, crying that nothing should take precedence over the face of Jesus.

So it should be with us. That's why we gather to remember.